Financial Empowerment:
Realign Your Finances to God's Will

PAMELA CARMICHAEL

LIVING
SUCCESS
PUBLISHERS

Published by LIVING SUCCESS PUBLISHERS

ISBN (paperback): 978-0-9917850-0-1
ISBN (ebook): 978-0-9917850-1-8

Printed in the United States of America

This book will help you to:

* Recognize that God is the Ultimate Source for every need in your life
* Identify the reasons for the financial challenges you face
* Apply God's solution to improve your personal finances
* Identify and appreciate the benefits of doing things God's way
* Bless yourself and others through the practice of Godly financial principles
* Shatter the perception or stronghold that God does not delight in your prosperity
* Take steps towards financial freedom

With His will in mind as you manage your finances, God will empower you. You will be able to:

* Attach eternal value to your money by funding ministries that spread the gospel, feed the hungry, educate and empower those who need hope and a future
* Bless yourself by being free financially, thus having little or no debt
* Make sound financial decisions knowing how to give, save, invest, or lend using Godly guidelines
* Change lives (yours, your family's and others) for good because God's wisdom will guide you
* Become the wealth creator and wealth distributor God intended you to be

DEDICATION

I dedicate this book to my daughter, Liane, who in her own way has stood by her mom throughout the process of writing this book. She has understood my desire to write and has looked forward with anticipation to the day when her mom's book would be printed and in her hand. May she also read and her understanding be enlightened.

I also dedicate this book to my sisters and brothers, who have struggled financially following the recent market upheavals that have caught many by surprise; and to those who for various reasons have found rising above a certain financial threshold to be challenging. I pray that this book will be more than an encouragement to you—in fact, a means by which the Lord moves you into your financial destiny. May the best of His blessing be yours as you serve Him faithfully in heart, in word, in deed, and in your finances.

CONTENTS

ACKNOWLEDGMENTS

I extend heartfelt thanks to all who in some way—whether through prayers, financial help, emotional support, or other—helped me to produce this book. You are the gifts of God to me to help me reach my destiny. Thank you, all.

Frank Goviea—my first supporter and one willing to help along the way through reviews and prayers.

Dr. Samuel H. Donkor—Senior Pastor of All Nations Full Gospel Church, Toronto, Canada for giving the "go ahead" to write this book.

Sandra Prince—for your contribution as a supporter of anything I do. God bless you.

Hyacinth Mwila—a friend and a sister indeed. Thank you for always showing an interest in the book and its progress.

Rosemond Mawugbe—I know you prayed for me along the way. Thanks for putting in the hard work prayer requires and for believing in me.

Jesus Christ—my Saviour and Lord, through whose strength I was able to complete this project. All honour and glory belongs to Him.

CHAPTER 1

Why Money?

Why is money such an important topic today? Everyday activities revolve around money. We can't do much without it. Money also shows the intents and contents of our hearts as well as our attitudes toward God and others. Money is important because it can have eternal value.

The Bible provides God's solution to man's sin problem. As believers we know that Christ has saved us from sin and eternal death, given us eternal life, delivered us from sin's bondage, healed us physically and emotionally, and given us countless blessings. Yet many Christians do not see Christ as the solution to their financial problems. Though the Word of God says much about money and promises that God will meet the needs of His children; many struggle in this area of their lives. As believers, this ought not to be.

If the Word of God is our compass throughout our Christian walks, why do we not heed its advice when it comes to our finances? If we so believe God and His promises, why do we not heed His instructions in this area?

In one or more areas of their lives, Christians have difficulty obeying God's Word regarding money, whether it is to tithe, to give, to count the cost, to use money and not to serve it, or to be wise stewards. If Christians became free of money—understanding and knowing how to handle it correctly—their lives would greatly improve. Not only would positive changes emerge in their financial positions, but their correct view of money would be reflected in their relationships with the Lord.

SO WHY TALK ABOUT MONEY?

Money Is Personal

No one on this earth is unaffected by this resource called money. Almost everything we need in life finds its value or weight in this resource. It is—without a doubt—the currency everyone carries. Some people tell us that money is unimportant, but as long as we are on this side of life, money will have a role in our lives. We may have a lot, just enough, barely enough, or none at all. For each of those levels, money will have some effect on us. We will worry about having too much, not having enough to meet our needs, or want more for us, our families, and others around us.

Money affects every life. Money is a personal thing.

Money Answers All Things

The Word of God says that the Lord has given us, His children, all things pertaining to life and godliness. I believe that includes money. We also know that money answers all things – there is little that can be accomplished without the use of money. 'All things' includes things like food, clothing, education, health care, and spiritual life. 'All things' is related to the physical as well as the spiritual. We may ask, "How can 'all things' be spiritual?" Money pays to maintain our church buildings, to source teaching materials and office supplies, to send us to conferences, and to provide other resources to build us up in the faith. As the writer of Ecclesiastes 10:19 says, "A feast is made for laughter, and wine makes merry; but money answers everything" (emphasis added).

Money Is Good, Not Evil

After all these years of reading the Bible, many still think money is evil; however, the Word of God tells us that the love of money, not money itself, is the root of all evil (1 Timothy 6:10). Money is good if used but not loved. Often many make the fatal mistake of loving money rather than God and His people. Some Christians are afraid of money simply because they fear it will control them. Others downplay its importance in their lives and in building the kingdom of God.

For money to remain a valuable resource, you must master it, see its usefulness, and use it effectively. If you see money this way, you won't 'fall in love' with it, get greedy, or hoard it. But you will find good uses for it.

Money is good and useful.

Money Is a Servant (a Tool)

If we view money as a tool the Master has placed in our hands, we will learn to use it better. Money doesn't function on its own; it needs human intervention to bring about its usefulness. God puts money in our hands to serve as an instrument of blessing not only to us but also to others. Money is available to serve our interests as well as God's. We need to employ money to work for us and the kingdom of God.

Just as money in the hands of the righteous can bring about good, so money in the hands of the wicked can promote evil. Hence, the Enemy fights or wars against every believer who desires to bless and promote God's work with his or her money. He fights by convincing many to spend their money foolishly and, as a result, become bound by consumer debt. Sometimes he creates problems that cause them to easily lose their money.

If you remain alert to the Enemy's devices and are proactive, you will be able to have more than enough money to do good. Money stands ready and waiting for you to use it to do good. Use it well.

Money Is a By-product of You

Usually those who are not out looking for money make lots of it. Let me explain. The most successful or wealthy people are those who enjoy what they do. They are the kind of people who create a product or service because they believe in it; they fully believe it will benefit those who use it and, as such, never consider that the product or service might not sell. These people live on purpose for a purpose, and out of their driven lives, they must do something outstanding that brings the benefit of financial abundance. They are not necessarily top grade-A students, but they have a gift or idea they followed through on and made money from. They are paid for who they are, what they do well, and what they really enjoy doing. I believe the energy they put into what they do, along with effective marketing, causes their products and services to stand out above the rest.

Have you ever realized that some products stand out more than others? Some brand names are household names more than others, even though other brand names sell the same or better product or service. If you investigate the stories of the people behind these products, you will often find a love for doing what they do, doing it well, and promoting it no matter what led to money in their hands.

Clearly, life is more than money, and money is

merely a by-product of who you are. As the Word says, your gift will make room for you before great men (Proverbs 18:16). Money is a by-product of carrying out your life's purpose.

Money Can Have Eternal Value

Yes, this may sound a bit strange, but money does have eternal value. As we discussed earlier, money is a tool God has placed in our hands to do good. The good it does can be either temporal or eternal.

Think about this. When you give to your local church, you participate in God's business of spreading the gospel. Through the spreading of the gospel people give their lives to Christ; here you can see the eternal value. Some complain that all the church wants is money, but remember, money answers all good things. You can attach eternal value to your money when you give to your local church or missions, or when you sponsor a child, fund someone's education, or send a preacher to plant a church. How will someone hear the good news unless someone is sent (Romans 10:14-15)? How can someone be sent without financial support of the local church? Money has eternal value when it is used to spread the good news.

WHAT TO EXPECT IN THIS BOOK

As you walk through the pages of this money book, I will discuss various aspects of financial management. You can see the areas of financial management I plan to cover from this perspective:

* Good money management brings positive returns: income generation, tithing, saving, investing, giving, and lending.

* Bad money management leads to negative returns: excessive spending and borrowing.

I will highlight the problems we face in each of these areas based on personal experience, observation, and research. We will also discuss some of the reasons for these problems, which are often a reflection of our relationship with God. Certainly we will delve into the Word of God and find the solution to each problem.

Although most solutions will be biblical, I will provide some practical tips to help you along this rocky financial road some have been experiencing. Certainly you will learn that God's Word, when rightly applied, will benefit you in every aspect of your Christian walk, including your finances. For certain, if you govern your life including your money matters according to the Word of God, you will by all means be successful and prosperous.

I wrote this book to enlighten, educate, and

empower the body of Christ to be knowledgeable, understanding, and wise in the use of the money resources God has entrusted to us.

One of the challenges we face is the lack of finances common among many Christians. For me this was a problem for years as I observed Christians struggling through life because they lacked the necessary financial resources. Much more can be accomplished to spread the gospel of Christ, but lack of finances and the unwillingness of many to give hinder the progress of God's work.

This book seeks to address why this lack exists and what is needed to bring financial increase. Of great importance is understanding how to use the financial increase God provides to bless the kingdom of God. To learn that, we must place eternal value on the money available for our use.

This book calls the body of Christ to get its financial house in order. This is a call to start living as children of God, not orphans or beggars. It's a call to examine our hearts and attitudes toward God and what He has entrusted to us. It's a call to use what we have to be a blessing and build the kingdom of God.

When you finish reading this book, my prayer is not that you will say this was a good or powerful book. My prayer is that you will act to change how you handle your finances. I hope you will become stronger in your walk with the Lord. His grace will give you the ability to change the way you manage your finances and align them to His will.

Get ready for financial empowerment God's way! As you examine His Word, may He give you the grace to obey, for this obedience will lead to His blessing on your life.

Special Bonus Offer

You will receive a FREE complementary e-course:

5 Tips to Financial Empowerment God's Way

It's not enough just to have this book in hand, read it and move on without implementing some of what you learned here. You have to continue on the road to Godly financial empowerment. In this free e-course, I will walk you through some action steps that lead to good money management that will bring positive returns into your finances and your life.

Get your copy now at:

http://www.pamelavcarmichael.com/financial-empowerment/5-tips-ecourse

Note: This ebook is NOT free to sell or give away to others. Thanks for understanding.

CHAPTER 2

God is the Source

We need to realign our thinking and stop seeing God as limited in His ability to provide. Our thoughts need to be renewed through the Word to move us out of a poverty mentality into knowing and believing that we can prosper. A blessed man is a prosperous man.

The earth is the Lord's, and all its fullness, the world and those who dwell therein. For He has founded it upon the seas, and established it upon the waters.

—Psalm 24:1–2

It is perfectly logical to assume that a wise and competent Creator would provide for the needs of His creatures in their various stages of growth.

—Charles Fillmore, Prosperity

SO WHO IS OUR SOURCE?

Have we ever asked ourselves, Who is my source? If not, now is a good time to do so. So, who is our source? Is it our job or business income—or is it God? Money is such a personal thing that we often fail to recognize that the money we hold in our hands is not ours.

Perhaps you work hard and deserve to be paid for your services. However, you may think your education, talent, creativity, good opportunities, or even your good looks brought what you have.

But again, I ask, Who is your source? Being a good Christian, you may likely answer that God is your source, but do you really believe that?

I've had to ask myself this question a few times in my life—when money seemed limited, when I had to juggle figures to see how I could best meet my needs when no money seemed to be in sight, yet bills were due. I've even asked this question when times were good and I enjoyed abundance.

So who is your source when times are good and all seems well but trouble comes and all your savings and income suddenly dry up? Do you trust God only when you have enough or live in abundance? Or do you trust Him even when you don't know where the money is coming from?

WHY WE DON'T TRUST GOD AS OUR SOURCE

What causes us not to trust God as our source? What are some of the effects of limiting God and not seeing Him as our source?

We Don't Think We Will Prosper

Our life's experiences have affected the way we think about our God, the Creator and our heavenly Father. The distorted thinking of some Christians has caused them to believe they will never prosper. The self talk of many is that nothing will ever work well for them—in their workplace, business, finances, ministry, or personal relationships. Yet the Bible says that whatever we do shall prosper (Ps. 1:3). When nothing works, our faith in God dwindles and sometimes dies completely. We fail to realize that we believed more in our failure than in the Word of God. If our expectation is that nothing we do will prosper, then nothing will. But if our expectation is that we will prosper, then we will. Our faith must match our words and actions. Then God will meet us at the level of our expectations.

We Don't Believe His Word

Usually the problem is that our talk and actions do match our inward beliefs. Though we say that we trust God to meet all our needs, we don't really believe this. We don't think God is able to do what He says in His

Word. Our faith in God is fickle when it comes to trusting Him to provide for us, and this fickleness is most evident when we face troubled times. We pray much and say we believe God, but when we leave our closets and go back to the world/reality, we allow the circumstances around us to overwhelm us with defeating thoughts. Our thoughts and actions prove that we don't trust Him. We take matters into our own hands—which usually results in things getting worse. Part of trusting God as our source means asking Him for direction, but often we go ahead and do what we think is best without consulting God and/or seeking the wise counsel of those He has placed around us.

Worry Is Our Friend

Worry is often the companion of many believers. It's just proof of our lack of faith in God. Worry shows that we believe more in our circumstances than in our God. We constantly worry about how to meet our obligations or where the next meal will come from—or we create negatives about how hard getting our next job will be. The Lord admonishes us not to worry about anything, but to pray and give thanks to Him (Phil. 4:6–7). But we worry, and as such, we have no peace of mind and become irritable with our loved ones instead of enjoying the blessings we do have. If we took heed to God's Word, we would have peace in the midst of every storm, whether financial or not. This peace would keep us from being anxious.

We Have In-the-Box Thinking

Being overly anxious or worried not only brings inner turmoil but also creates in-the-box thinking that affects our lives. When our financial problems so consume and overwhelm us, we cannot think clearly. This in-the-box thinking prevents us from seeing beyond our problem and causes us to believe more in the problem than in God. Instead of focusing on God and His promises and on serving Him, our minds and hearts are tied up with our problems.

If we heed His Word, let go, and let Him have His way—releasing all to Him through prayer and supplication—He will open doors of provision for us. When we seek God in prayer and give thanks to Him in advance of seeing our needs met, we will experience not only peace but a peace that protects our minds and hearts. With Christ guarding our minds and with our hearts open to Him, we are in a position to receive direction from Him. God will open our eyes to see the opportunities around us, through which God will provide. With our minds and hearts guarded, God will show us the 'acre of diamonds' we are sitting on, through which He will make His provision real to us. Yes, we are sitting on our own acre of diamonds—we just don't know it.

We Feel Like We Should Be Among the Poor

When we focus on the effects of poverty in the world or

on the seemingly personal lack we are experiencing, we often lose sight of God's unlimited supply. This again goes back to our way of thinking. Like unbelievers, Christians question the suffering of others and themselves and resign themselves to living among the many poor. We may not realize that this imbalanced world—many poor and few rich—has everything to do with man's attitude toward money and power rather than with God's ability to provide. The God of all creation has provided for His creatures. He has not left us to fend for ourselves; rather, He made provision for us even before He created us. We therefore need to believe that God will continue to be our source and bless us so we may be a blessing to others, including the poor among us.

We See Ourselves, Not God, as the Source

Some have the attitude that what they have is theirs because they worked hard for it. "It's my money, I earned it" is the attitude, even of believers. This type of attitude leads to a lack of faith in God and a dependence on self.

Please take a reality check. Did you come and create this world, or were you born into it? Did you create the earth, the moon and stars, and all else that exists? When you examine the vastness of this world, not just earth, how do you measure up? Have you given yourself daily breath and strength? Do you determine the number of your days? Even your very breath is from God, your source. Your education, talent, and whatever else you possess came to you not because you created it, but because God gave it to you. All that you have is God's; you don't own anything. Everything belongs to God, including you and me. You are His steward of His possessions. The earth and everything and everyone living on it belong to the Lord.

Clearly your thoughts must align with God's Word for you to fully recognize that He is your source and that everything you need is in Him and from Him. Until you seek God in prayer and daily feed on His Word to destroy these negative views, you'll walk through life saved from sin but bound in your thoughts and other areas of your life. Please try to develop a healthy view of God and totally trust Him as your source.

TRUSTING GOD AS OUR SOURCE

By definition a source is any thing or place from which something comes, arises, or is obtained; origin (See http://dictionary.reference.com/browse/source?s=t). God is the origin from which all life flows. Psalm 24:1 says that the earth belongs to God, everything in it and everyone who lives on it. All is God's (Deut. 10:14; Job 41:11; Ps. 50:12; 89:11).

So how do you view your God? Is He the origin of all you need? Is He the One from whom your needs will be met daily? Or do you still think He is limited in His ability to provide for you? If so, you need to examine the

Word and see how you can align your will to God's Word and fully understand that He is your source.

* God, the Creator, prepared for the needs of His children beforehand. From the beginning, the One who created us has been the source of all our needs. First, He designed this world for us to live in. In His love for us, He planted a garden with food, clothing, water, shelter, gold, and precious stones. The sin of Adam brought upon us the curse of hard work and poverty—by the sweat of our brows we eat (Gen. 3:17–20). But faithful as He is, God did not take away His provision from us. From creation until now we see His faithfulness in providing for all who live on this earth.

* Moreover, for those who believe and confess Christ as Lord and Savior, His Word promises over and over again that He will take care of all our needs and grant the desires of our hearts (Ps. 21:2; 37:4). Yet when we face financial difficulties, we often become fearful and think God's resources have dried up. We always need to remember that God is the source of all our needs.

* "As His divine power has given to us all things that pertain to life and godliness, through the knowledge of Him who called us by glory and virtue" (2 Peter 1:3). What a wonderful promise! God has given you more than you need to enjoy life and live a godly life before Him. God wants to give you not just enough but more than enough to be a blessing to others.

Second Corinthians 9:8 says that God will cause you to have more than you need so you can give toward good works. The Word of God emphasizes that God will supply both what you need in your life today and what you need for the future. Regardless of your need, God gives to you when you ask. The Father God knows what you need and will provide (Matt. 6:31–32).

* If God has taken the time and effort to number the hairs on each person's head, don't you think He has all the details of your life worked out (Luke 12:7)? If He has not only given great care to determine how many hairs are on your head, but has also numbered each of them; don't you think He knows what your financial position is? He has said that you are more valuable to Him than many sparrows. He takes care of the animals, but He takes greater care of every human being created in His image. God had all your needs figured out long before you knew about them, so don't worry.

* "And my God shall supply all your need according to His riches in glory by Christ Jesus." Yes, you probably know Philippians 4:19 all too well. If God says He will, then He will. Scripture is filled with promise after promise that God will take care of you. The psalmist said that as a youth and throughout his years on earth, he did not see the righteous and their children beg for food (Ps. 37:25). The righteous includes you! You and your children shall never beg for food because God in His faithfulness as the

source of all good things will provide for you.

TRUST HIM

In this world, relying on ourselves alone is signing up for certain failure. God has promised in His Word that He will meet our needs and provide for us along life's journey. If we trust Him, He will surely make life good for us. If we trust Him, we will have peace regardless of the turmoil going on around us. When hope fails for others, our trust in God will keep the hope in us alive, and we will see nothing as impossible or hopeless. If we trust Him, we will always remember that He who promised us many blessings is faithful to perform the word He spoke to His people. When we trust God as our source, we will experience not only His peace but also His provision.

Remember, the starting point of all you have, all you need, all you will possess, and all you will be in life is God. He is the stream from which all things flow. Your income is not the starting point of your provision. God is.

Feeling Boxed In?

Anytime you feel financially boxed in, take a walk or go for a ride in your car. Look up at the sky and view the scenery around you. Does anything seem lacking? The Painter of the sky, the Creator and Designer of the earth, is your Father. If He has so fittingly provided for this earth and the many billions of people who live on it, remind yourself that He has provided for you. God is your source.

CHAPTER 3

Create Wealth:
God Has Given You the Power

Many see work as drudgery or hardship. They consider it a necessary evil. In these days, society is more interested in how to get something for nothing. For many, working has come to be more of a chore than a pleasure. As Christians, however, we must learn that work is a gift from God and a means by which we create and distribute wealth. We need to realign our thinking to God's and see work as a priority like He does.

And you shall remember the Lord your God, for it is He who gives you power to get wealth, that He may establish His covenant which He swore to your fathers, as it is this day.

—Deuteronomy 8:18

He shall be like a tree planted by the rivers of water, that brings forth its fruit in its season, whose leaf also shall not wither; and whatever he does shall prosper.

—Psalm 1:3

WHAT IS WEALTH?

Misconception of Wealth

What is wealth anyway? Does wealth mean having millions and billions of dollars all for ourselves, or is there more to it than that? We keep wondering what wealth is. What is God's meaning of wealth or riches or prosperity? Why is the Bible filled with so many examples of those who were wealthy? If we take a close look at the stories of the godly men and women in the Bible, we'll see that they not only walked with God, but also were wealthy in possessions and successful in whatever work they did.

In Christianity today talking about wealth or money is still considered a taboo for some. If we do talk about having more than enough, being wealthy, or being successful in our careers, we tend to do so with much timidity. Many have an inward fear that success or wealth is not God's will for us. Also, we don't want to disappoint ourselves if we fail at creating wealth. Furthermore, we wouldn't want to be considered unspiritual for wanting more than enough. Yet God longs to bless His children with more than enough not only for themselves but also for the benefit of others.

The wealth some tend to shy away from having is wealth God willingly gives us the power or ability to attain. Deuteronomy 8 cautioned Israel so that when they had made it to the Promised Land they wouldn't become puffed up with pride, thinking that all their strength and might had caused them to attain wealth. In this passage (Deut. 8:11–13, 17–18), God describes wealth and the purpose of it:

Beware that you do not forget the Lord your God by not keeping His commandments, His judgments, and His statutes which I command you today, lest—when you have eaten and are full, and have built beautiful houses and dwell in them; and when your herds and your flocks multiply, and your silver and your gold are multiplied, and all that you have is multiplied; when your heart is lifted up, and you forget the Lord your God who brought you out of the land of Egypt, from the house of bondage. . . . Then you say in your heart, "My power and the might of my hand have gained me this wealth." And you shall remember the Lord your God, for it is He who gives you power to get wealth, that He may establish His covenant which He swore to your fathers, as it is this day (emphasis added).

How God Defines Wealth?

So, according to Scripture, wealth is having all we need and more. It is having abundance of food and clothing, beautiful houses to live in, prosperity in work, financial increase, and multiplication of all we have. Biblically, wealth means strength, might, power, and excess; in short, it is having more than enough. We cannot define wealth with a number, although many would say that wealthy people are those who have millions and billions of dollars. Wealth is having over and above what we need or desire; it is all-round prosperity and success.

But I think we often overlook another part to being wealthy. Why does God give wealth? Does He simply want us to be comfortable and keep it all for ourselves? God said that He gave wealth to Israel to establish His covenant with them, the one He made with their forefathers starting with Abraham. God promised Abraham that he and his descendants would be blessed and be a blessing to all the families of the earth (Gen. 12:1–3). He reiterated this covenant to Isaac and Jacob, and today through Christ we are partakers of this same covenant (Gal. 3:13–14). God willingly blesses us in every way so we may be a blessing to others. As we continue into the upcoming chapters, we will learn ways in which we can become a blessing to others.

The Ultimate Source of Wealth

But how do we attain this wealth? Again, Deuteronomy 8 gives us the answer. Although we derive wealth through work (our strengths, skills, knowledge), work is not the source of any wealth we attain. God warned Israel not to consider themselves the powerhouse of their wealth. Truly work is the means through which we receive financial reward for our work; however, God and God alone is the One who gives wealth. The ultimate source of wealth is God, and through work or productivity God provides wealth to us.

THE PROBLEM WITH WORK

Though work is the main avenue through which wealth is created, some Christians hold an unbiblical or negative view of work. These opinions of work limit the blessings and joy God wants us to experience in our lives. Here are some of the misconceptions we possess about work that hinder God's anointing on our lives to create wealth:

My Work Has Nothing to Do with God

We disconnect from God whatever work we do that generates income. At least two schools of thought are at play here: (1) God is not interested in what we do, or (2) we proudly think that what we have is from our own strength and wisdom (Deut. 8:17). Both of these misconceptions cause us to lose the desire to involve God in our daily business activities.

My Work Feels like a Curse

Due to living in a fallen world, we often misinterpret work as a curse. Many think God is punishing them with work, especially when they don't like what they're doing.

I Spend Too Much Time Working

We complain that we work more than we relax or play. We have this misconception that we should spend less time working and more time relaxing. Get-rich-quick schemers often promote this train of thought. They play on our desire for more and our dislike of work.

I Work Just to Pay the Bills

We see work as a necessary evil rather than seeing the good it brings. Sometimes we find ourselves complaining about the people we work with, the pay that isn't enough, and the working conditions that aren't as nice as we would wish. We miss acknowledging the blessings we and others receive from our work.

I Don't Like Working

Whoa! That's a big one. Some don't like what they do on a daily basis. If they aren't talking about how much they hate work, they're shirking going to work or doing the required minimum because (again) it just pays the bills.

WHY WORK? GOD'S PERSPECTIVE

"So why do I have to work?" This is a question we may sometimes ask, especially when we don't feel like working. According to an old saying, work is never complete. Yes, something always needs to be done, whether at home, in our business or place of employment, even when we're on vacation. Work is a very necessary part of life because it is part of who God is. We are created in His image, and like Him we are workers.

Work Originated with God

God created the world not by dreaming, wishing, imagining, or relaxing—but by working. The world we see now would not exist if God hadn't done the work of creation. God knew what He wanted the world to look like and went through the effort to create it and maintain it. After creating this world, He approved of the results of His work and said it was very good (Gen. 1:31). All that we experience—the seasons, the stars, the sun, the moon, and all the planets—are the results of God's work.

This introduction to God in Genesis shows us that God not only envisions what He wants, but also works to make it become a reality. Since work is part of God's nature and we have been created in His image, work is also part of our nature. God has created us to work. We are His masterpiece, His special work He created, but we are also His coworkers (Eph. 2:10). God loves to work, and He loves to see His creation at work. He gives each person his or her own work to do and is pleased with our activity.

Work Is God's Priority

God created the heavens and earth in six days, and on the seventh day He rested (Gen. 2:1–3). In the Law He gave to the Israelites, He commanded them to work six days and rest on the Sabbath (Ex. 23:12). By this example God showed us the importance of work. We should spend the largest part of our lifetimes productively. Think about it. We should spend six out of seven days each week working; that is approximately 85 percent of our time at work. In His wisdom God understands that the work of creating or building dispenses a lot of energy from us; therefore He instructs us to take time to rest and be refreshed. But, as we can see, work was—and still is—the priority for God and man.

We also see work at the top of God's priorities when He created Adam. God immediately put Adam to work. His assignments included ruling the earth (Gen. 1:28), taking care of the garden of Eden (Gen. 2:28), and naming the animals (Gen. 2:19). Adam was born to work. God could have named the animals Himself, but He gave the assignment to Adam. God could have filled the earth with many more human beings without Adam and Eve, but He chose to work with man. He gave man the work to produce and reproduce, to fill the earth and manage it, and to take authority over every living creature in it. God wanted Adam to exercise his dominion right away through working and experiencing the joy of working. What God did showed Adam that through work we can solve problems, produce good results, and enjoy fulfillment.

Work Brings Reward

Psalm 128:2 says, "You will eat the fruit of your labor; blessings and prosperity will be yours" (NIV). Through work God makes provision for us. From the work we do, we will need to eat; however, if we choose not to work, then we shouldn't eat (2 Thess. 3:10). God gives us the responsibility to take care of our families and is displeased if we fail to work and provide for them (1 Tim. 5:8). He uses work as a means of provision for us and our families. In addition, work relieves us from being dependent on others and becoming a financial burden to our relatives or society (1 Thess. 2:9; 2 Thess. 3:8).

So work does more than just pay the bills. When we are able to use our strengths, skills, experience and knowledge to work and receive compensation for it, this is a blessing from God. We don't just receive money for our labor. In fact, we receive food, clothing and shelter, as well as the benefits of health insurance, life and disability insurance, pension contributions, and more. Work is an extension of God's hand on us to bless us; therefore, we should be thankful.

Work Is for God and Honors God

Bondservants, be obedient to those who are your masters according to the flesh, with fear and trembling, in sincerity of heart, as to Christ; not with eyeservice, as men-pleasers, but as bondservants of Christ, doing the will of God from the heart, with goodwill doing service, as to the Lord, and not to men, knowing that whatever good anyone does, he will receive the same from the Lord, whether he is a slave or free.

—Ephesians 6:5–8

Whether we are employees, those who are self-employed, business owners, or investors, our work should honor God. The main focus of our work should be to please God, not men, and to work knowing God is present with us at all times. Why? Because the Lord rewards the work we do and how we do it.

We are sometimes unaware of things we do that displease God. We sometimes steal time—we're tardy to work or fail to adhere to the contract we agreed to. Sometimes we fail to give our best and provide disappointing results, then we wonder why we didn't get the promotion we wanted.

Whatever we do in life should be pleasing to God. Daily we should ask God to give us the ability to do our work well and let it honor Him. Joseph was a great example of one who honored God in his work. Even as a slave, his superiors saw that God was with him and blessed everything he did. Joseph had the spirit of excellence upon him, and others saw this at each stage of his life. Regardless of what they believe, people should be able to see that same spirit of excellence in us and be willing to trust and favor us.

Whether at work or in relaxation, our lives as Christians should honor God.

Colossians 3:17 says, "And whatever you do in word or deed, do all in the name of the Lord Jesus, giving thanks to God the Father through Him." No disconnect should exist between you, your work, and God. God is interested in all of you. The thought that your work is separate from your relationship with God dishonors Him. The attitude that your strength and wisdom, not God, are what provide for you also dishonors Him.

Any credit, any good in our lives, is from the Lord; we therefore need to guard against pride that rises up in our hearts when we achieve success and prosperity through our work. God, who cares for us, is the One who gives us the ability to create wealth.

Work Is God's Assignment to Us

Work was part and parcel of ruling over the earth, and every assignment God gave Adam required work (Gen. 1:26-28; 2:19; Ps. 8:4-8). Likewise every assignment or task given to all who follow after Adam, including us, requires work. Work is an essential part of who we are.

Work is necessary to living out God's will for our lives. Building the ark God used to keep Noah, his family and the animals safe took work. Noah worked to build it. Gifted in administration and endowed with a big dream, Joseph had to work. Moses's assignment to deliver Israel required work. To lead the children of Israel into the Promised Land required effort on Joshua's part to be an effective leader. Jesus came to do the work Father God had sent Him to do—to preach the gospel to the poor, to heal the broken hearted, to declare freedom to the captives, and to open the eyes of the blind. It all required work. Every assignment God gave them was the fulfillment of His purpose for their lives. Their willingness to do the work brought blessings to them and others.

Your assignment from God may not be as grand as those mentioned above, but it will still require work for successful completion. You may be a father or mother who provides for your household. You may be a teacher responsible for educating the future generation. Maybe you're in the corporate world, providing products and services locally or to the world at large. Whatever your assignment is, it will require work. Spiritual, mental, and physical effort will be required to complete whatever assignment you have in life.

We often fail to see the blessing of work because the effort, sweat, or toil of it blinds us. Some think work is a punishment or curse from God, rather than a gift from God to be enjoyed (Eccl. 5:18–19). Once we are sure God wants us to work where we are, we should accept the gift, take it seriously, and do the work that pleases Him.

Work Leads to Wealth Distribution

Work is the means through which we create wealth, and wealth creation leads to wealth distribution. In biblical terms, God gives us the power to create wealth so we can be blessed and be a blessing to others. Therefore all the wealth we create is not for us alone, but for others. The promise God made to Abraham, Isaac, and Jacob has passed to us through Jesus Christ. We, the seed of Abraham, are blessed and are to bless.

God's covenant is reciprocal (Gen. 12:1–2; Deut. 8:18) in that God has blessed us to be wealth creators, and through this God empowers us to be wealth distributors. But what does wealth distribution mean or involve? As wealth distributors, we take some of the wealth we have created and give or lend it to others, either through our education, gifts, skills, or money. God wants us to take every blessing He has given to us and use it to bless others. As wealth distributors, God empowers us to do the following:

∗ Support church ministry. Paul instructed the Corinthians to set aside money weekly to give toward their sister church's needs. He also applauded the church at Philippi for generous giving. You can support some area of your church's ministry, such as an outreach program, youth ministry, food bank, or some other aspect of the work as God directs you.

∗ Send out missionaries. Although giving toward

missions may be seen as part of church ministry support, it is a very special aspect of it. While we can't go to certain places, our money can support those who are willing to go into the remote parts of the world to preach the gospel. This can be one of our contributions to reaching the lost for Christ.

✳ Give to other charitable or worthy causes. The world has many needs, and we are an extension of God's hands and an expression of His love to this suffering world. When we distribute wealth to sponsor a child, giving them much-needed food, clothing, and shelter, we show God's love. When disaster strikes, we can be the first on hand to help by providing clothing, medication, water, and whatever is called for. Also in our own country we can contribute to a children's hospital and donate to cancer research.

Through this wealth distribution we affect the lives of others, whether they belong to the household of faith or not. Our work as wealth distributors will cause others to see the light and give praises to God (Matt. 5:16). Also when they see God's blessing on our lives, they will want to come with us into our Father's house (Is. 55:5; Zec. 8:23). Our wealth creation and distribution will be a witness of God's goodness and greatness.

We can give out of what we have; from the financial reward we gain from our work, God expects us to give to support the needs of others. The church at Macedonia helped sister churches in need through giving from their substance (2 Cor. 8:1–4). In Ephesians 4:28, Paul clearly points out that the one who is able to work and create wealth is in a good position to give to those in need.

Not only does our creating wealth have a positive impact on society, but the actual work is also a means of wealth distribution. The daily work we perform touches people's lives through products created or services rendered. For example, a doctor aids in healing the sick, a money manager helps people keep their finances in order, and a factory worker creates products bought by customers who need them. Our work and wealth are all part of the wealth creation and distribution process. We should use what we have to be a blessing to others.

SO HOW DO WE CREATE WEALTH?

We have discussed the importance of viewing work from God's perspective. We know work is a priority for God and should be so for us as well. If we want to achieve success, we need to embrace God's perspective of work as our own. With this as a starting point, our goals should be to know and function by God's working standards while creating wealth. Our attitude toward work and how we work are of equal importance to God. Therefore, we should be aware of His principles and practice them if we want to succeed in creating wealth.

God's Power and Presence (God's Anointing)

One thing we should all seek if we want success is the

presence and anointing of God, be it while we're doing our work, being a parent, or managing our finances. Regardless of what we do, we need God's anointing.

Just as the Lord did for Bazalel and others who worked on the construction of the tabernacle, He can do for you (Ex. 31:1–6). Ask the Lord, and He will fill you "with the Spirit of God, in wisdom, in understanding, in knowledge, and in all manner of workmanship" (Ex. 31:3).

Joseph's story reminds us that no matter what stage of life we are in, no matter what our position or social status may be, if we have the Lord's presence with us, we will be favored, promoted, and prosperous in our work. From pit to palace, Joseph's life displays that the presence of God is paramount to our success in work and life. Being ever conscious of God's presence and anointing on our lives will keep us in the right attitude, even when life isn't going well. Joseph's work—to administer, organize, govern, interpret, and discern—in Potiphar's house and in prison meshed with God's presence and anointing and made room for Joseph to become the second-in-command over a nation.

Like Joseph, you can experience similar successes. In your work, you too can be successful. Honor God in all you do, and those in authority over you will see that the hand of the Lord is on you. Ask the Lord for favor and promotion. Seek the Lord's help to do your work with excellence, to serve well, and to make your work prosper. At the beginning of your day, invite God to go with you and before you to make your day prosperous. For your sake, He will bless those who do business with you because you are His child. Because of you, people will be at ease to do business with you and let you take care of their business. They will have complete confidence in you because they will see that the Lord is with you.

With God's presence and His anointing on your work, you can receive promotion and reap financial blessings from your work.

Obedience to God

Wealth is created out of obedience. Like his father, Abraham, Isaac walked in obedience to God. God told Abraham to leave the familiar and comfortable and to go to a place he didn't know. His obedience caused him to be more prosperous. He attributed his wealth to the blessings of God on his life (Gen. 24:35).

Then to his son Isaac the Lord once again gave a hard instruction—to do the illogical and stay where famine and economic downturn existed, to stay where he was likely to struggle or starve.

Imagine God asking you to stay where hardship existed, especially with a family to take care of. Isaac had a choice—either to believe God's promise or to move on. Out of obedience to God's Word, Isaac stayed, and in the time of famine when no one had the guts to expend their energy to plant anything, Isaac did. His act showed his faith in God to keep His promise of blessing. His obedience to God, while doing his work in the midst of hardship, brought blessing and prosperity (Gen. 26:12–14).

So how does this story apply to you today? Ask God for a listening ear to His voice and the ability to obey Him. Like Isaac, you need to listen closely to God so you may see opportunity, even during an economic downturn. You will require God's grace to step out in faith and do what others wouldn't dare. As you do so in obedience to God's Word, He will bring you success and prosperity. Every imaginable or unimaginable blessing can be yours if you have a relationship with Christ and live in obedience to His Word (Deut. 28:1–13). The work of your hands can prosper when you are in a right relationship with God (Ps. 1:1–3).

Joshua is another great example of success in work while obeying God. His responsibility to lead the people of Israel to finally possess the Promised Land was nothing short of daunting. God's instruction and encouragement to him in Joshua 1:7–9 are keys to our success and prosperity in life. The Word of God makes us strong and courageous in the face of work challenges. Having the Word as an integral part of our lives will give us the ability to prosper wherever we go and be successful in whatever work we do. Therefore, above all, obey the Word of God, and we will have good success.

Expect to Profit

One negative view some have of work is that it just pays the bills. In other words, we have just enough work and sometimes not enough to meet our needs. Though it is true that many are in debt or barely make enough to cover expenses due to the economic challenges we face, the Word of God says profit exists in all labor (Prov. 14:23). However, because of what economists predict, what we hear on the news, or our present and not-so-pleasant financial situation, our expectation is often lack and not financial increase and abundance.

Our attitude toward work affects the results of our work, whether it is profitable or not. One danger to avoid is having the wrong expectation—that we won't be profitable in work. The story in Luke 19:11–26 that describes the man with the one mina highlights some of the negative results of wrong expectations.

The one-mina man worked out of fear of his master; having done little with the mina (other than hiding it in a handkerchief), he brought no profit at all. We sometimes harbor hidden fears about our work— that we may lose our stream of income, that we will not get enough clients to make our business profitable, that the people we work with are hard and unreasonable, and that the money we receive won't be enough to meet our commitments.

If we work out of fear like the one-mina man, we will likely do the minimum work required. This is important because what we do with the resources we have determines the level of poverty vs. wealth or the level of failure vs. success we experience in our lives. Negative expectations result in two problems: we do the required minimum or make no profit from the little we do. Furthermore, our very actions and inner fears cause us to lose what we have to someone who already has more than we do. Both demotion and financial lack are the effects of wrong expectations.

The Lord says in Proverbs 14:23 that the work of a man's hands shall come back to him as a harvest. Whenever we work, we should expect a profit or reward for our labor. We must believe in our ability to do excellent work as well as in our Father's desire to bless us if we want be profitable. In the marketplace, no one builds a business or makes an investment without expecting a profit. As children of God, we should approach our work and lives knowing that whatever we do will prosper (Ps. 1:3). We are destined to prosper in all things (3 John 2).

Whatever you do, always expect that good will come from it (Phil. 4:8). If you want to get a good return from your work and have more than enough, then fill yourself with the Word of God and approach your work with a mind to succeed (Josh. 1:7–8). It is God's desire that you will prosper in all things, including receiving profit from the work you do; therefore, expect profit.

Work Diligently

While growing up, my mum encouraged me to work hard. Today we are told to work smart, not hard; however, God's Word encourages us to work diligently. We are expected to do the work and stick to it until it is completed; we should not consider giving up along the way. The book of Proverbs says much about being diligent and often draws a comparison between the hard worker and the lazy person.

Poverty is not a gift from God but the result of our actions. The actions of a lazy person will never lead to wealth. Lazy people are fearful of stepping out to do something and think their excuses are justifiable, yet they would rather relax or sleep than work. The lazy one never completes tasks; even feeding himself or herself proves to be a problem.

If you've ever been around lazy people, you've noticed that they are likely to know it all; they have an answer for everything (Prov. 26:13–16). Being lazy leads to hunger (Prov. 12:27; 19:15). Being lazy is awful because it brings poverty—poverty comes and invades your life and steals what you have (Prov. 24:30–34). Such need will lead lazy people to forced labor—working to pay the bills and get some food. Work is like a hard taskmaster to the lazy person, and you'll find that those who are diligent will have authority over the lazy (Prov. 12:24). Being lazy can destroy a person's life (Prov. 18:9). This is not the life God desires for any of His children.

Success in creating wealth is linked to being a diligent person. The price we gain for being diligent workers is riches, while the price we pay for laziness is lack (Prov. 10:4).

To be diligent in our work is not only financially rewarding but also personally satisfying (Prov. 13:4). When we are diligent and do excellent work, our performance makes room for us (Prov. 22:29). We are promoted, our work speaks for us, and prominent people want us to work with them or for them.

While having a day job, my friend started a jewelry-making business. She was very diligent at promoting her business and creating excellent pieces. This diligent work paid off, and some of her pieces were present in major shows across the country. This exposure made her become well known and sought after.

Regardless of your social status, educational level, or skill set, God wants you to work diligently. If you desire to create wealth that provides more than enough for you and your household, you will require diligence. No dream becomes a reality without lots of diligent work (Eccl. 5:3). If you work diligently, you will be one who rules and enjoys great blessings in life. The wealth of those who are lazy will be transferred to those who are diligent (see parable of the minas, Luke 19:13–26; parable of the talents, Matt. 25:14–29). Promotion and financial increase come to those who are diligent workers.

Use Time Wisely

Time is a gift from God. It is one of the many resources available to all human beings. In Ecclesiastes 9:11, the preacher tells us that time and chance happen to everyone. God does not give preferential treatment to a select few by giving them more time than others. He has given time to all, and we have the choice of what to do with the time He has given to us. We have twenty-four hours in a day, and what we do with them can determine our success or failure in creating wealth.

Time can neither be bought nor sold; it is priceless. You have time right now. Today is what matters. As you use time, each minute slips into eternity and is gone forever. You cannot gain it back. Every moment you are productive or unproductive is time that slips into eternity and is no more. Therefore, you must use the time God has given to you wisely.

A strong correlation exists between the effective use of time and your ability to create wealth. So what is your time worth? Does your time equate to a minimum wage per hour? Do you earn thousands or hundreds of thousands per year, or do you earn millions? This question isn't intended to discourage you, but to help you determine what you are doing with your time and whether you are doing enough.

No one starts out being a millionaire or having an immediate success story. The people we read about—the Warren Buffets, the Bill Gateses, the T. D. Jakeses, the

Michael Jordans, and the Thomas Edisons—all have a story to tell. They invested time and energy into what they loved (their dream) while working for small pay or no pay at all. But the time and effort they put into their dreams paid off—financially, socially, and in other ways. Their success came not only on account of their great gifts, talents, or other abilities, but also because of the time they put in and their readiness to seize God-given opportunities as they came.

So what are you doing with your time? You are accountable to God for the resources—time included—He has given to you. It doesn't matter whether you earn a low wage right now or whether your dream is to earn better pay or start a business of your own. What matters is what you are doing right now to prepare yourself for the opportunities God will send your way. Are you honing your skills? Are you studying in your field of interest? Are you learning about how to be a successful business owner and about the industry you want to operate in? Are you working diligently now to create wealth?

In your goal to create wealth, the time you have is precious and not to be wasted. As you discover the gifts God has given to you, make the best use of your time to enhance and cultivate them. Wealth is not "overnight success," but it comes in the process of time. If you use your time wisely working, grooming your skills, and educating yourself, you will be ready to seize the God-given opportunities that propel you to success and prosperity. Make the most of what you have—today.

Go the Extra Mile

In today's society, some find that doing more than is required is unappealing. Many want to receive maximum reward for minimum effort. Some want to get all they can for as little effort as possible, but success cannot be achieved in wealth creation or in life without putting in extra time or effort. Jesus said in Matthew 5:41, "And whoever compels you to go one mile, go with him two." Jesus calls us to walk in the extra-mile mode or to go beyond the call of duty. As Christians, we do extra when we give up our personal rights sometimes and give away more than someone asks for.

With work, as with giving or lending, we should be extra generous. We should do what is expected—and then more. We need to remember that in whatever work we do, we first and foremost do it as unto the Lord. If our mind-sets are such that our work is for God, then going the extra mile shouldn't be a problem.

So what is the extra mile? It could be working longer hours to finish a project on time. Maybe you do a task that is not normally part of your regular duties, or maybe the extra mile is helping a colleague with a challenging project. Whatever the extra mile may be for you, it will require more of your time, effort, energy, or expertise than usual.

I have gone the extra mile many times. On occasions I worked late hours to resolve issues so staff could start the next business day without delay. Other times I worked at home during evening hours to complete projects within specified timelines. Sometimes going the extra mile is necessary, and other times it is simply part of being who we are in Christ.

But what will be your benefit if you go the extra mile? I think the main benefit is that it glorifies your heavenly Father. Sure, you may receive a promotion, get a raise, or be acknowledged or appreciated for work well done, but no reward speaks louder than glorifying God. In the midst of giving glory to God because you do great work, going the extra mile opens the door for you as a witness of Christ.

Matthew 5:16 puts it this way: "Let your light so shine before men, that they may see your good works and glorify your Father in heaven." Doing good and extra work causes your light to shine before those you work with or do business with, drawing them closer to you to find God.

Multiple Streams of Income

Multiple streams of income (MSI) is a term used quite a bit lately. But what is MSI? Some think it means having more than one job—yes, some people do work several jobs—but MSI is defined not by having several jobs. Some of us can handle only one job because we have family commitments and other responsibilities that take priority. MSI, however, is a way of creating business systems that generate income without constant hands-on work. MSI is about turning a hobby into an income activity. It's about being creative, seeing a need, and being the supplier for that need—just like a business owner. MSI involves becoming a business instead of being part of someone else's business. It's about you becoming You, Inc., and conducting your personal and financial life as a business you manage with the purpose of making a profit. Being an MSI person involves using your activities, skills, education, interests, and money to create wealth.

Is this MSI business biblical? If you study the Bible, you won't find the term "multiple streams of income," but people did have different income streams. One interesting example is the Proverbs 31 woman. This woman is multifaceted—she is a wife, homemaker, and businesswoman. When you look at her business activities, you see that they encompass several streams— buying property, farming, making clothing—all with the intension of making a profit. She shines through as a great MSI earner. She is not idle but diligently works night and day to make profit from her ventures (Prov. 31:13, 15, 18–19, 27). Wow! Way to go, woman!

The benefits of having these multiple streams are evident—her husband doesn't worry about losing anything. She has enough to feed her household, she is able to help the poor, her family members are sufficiently clothed for the winter, and she has enough so she can dress in nice clothes too. But the benefits don't stop there—she does so well that the work she does speaks well of her (Prov. 31:31). Other examples of MSI earners are Paul, who ran a tent-making business while preaching the gospel, and Joseph, a carpenter who didn't depend solely on shepherding.

It is not my intention to have a lengthy discussion on this topic, but MSI is certainly something worth considering if you want to create wealth. So why should you consider MSI? In our society today, being an employee has one major drawback—the uncertainty of the job market due to the ongoing financial crisis. Along with this, the dependence on one stream of income leaves many uneasy and uncertain about their financial future and puts many in a bind. The Bible provides an example to us through the patriarchs and other men and women of faith—they were self-employed and didn't depend on only one stream of income. Unlimited in their capacity to earn income, they were therefore free to serve God without financial limitations.

Yes, part of serving God is using your wealth to promote and support the kingdom of God. Therefore, additional streams of income can benefit you in several ways:

* You can pay off your debt faster and live debt free. You can use money received through additional streams for the purpose of clearing long-term debt such as your mortgage or credit card bills. Being debt free will release you from worry that you lack sufficient funds to meet your commitments, literally breaking financial bondage. Living debt free will allow you to serve God more with your substance.

* You can create extra savings from additional streams of income. These savings may be used in specific ways—for example, for vacation or special gifting such as contributing to a special need or to the construction of a church, school, or hospital. You may even want to have a special savings fund for living expenses or unexpected expenses that arise (for example, car maintenance).

* You can give yourself a financial increase and reduce your dependence on one stream of income. This would relieve the underlying pressure or worry (not often spoken of to the family) if you are the main income earner.

* You can also use the extra income for investment purposes with the help of a good financial planner or investment advisor. Then you will have your money working to bring in more money.

* Having additional streams of income can also increase your level of personal satisfaction, especially when those extra streams involve the kind of work you like to do. Furthermore, when you are able to create something on your own that benefits you and your family, it brings a sense of fulfillment.

Now you can see a few ways you can use MSI to create wealth. If you have started and see the need to have at least one or two additional streams of income, then start acting now. Think about what you do now, what you like doing, and what needs you see around you that aren't being fulfilled. Consider how you can have a home business or personal service people would be willing to pay for. Like the Proverbs 31 woman, once you are certain your product or service is good, work on it even in the night season (Prov. 31:18). And remember that whatever you do will prosper.

BE HAPPY IN YOUR WORK

Work need not be so boring or terrible that you don't look forward to it. As we have discussed throughout this chapter, work is a gift from God and is meant to be a blessing to you. God created you to experience fulfillment through work. You shouldn't dread your work or try to find ways to avoid it. You should be looking forward to work every day.

I believe that if you are going to spend the majority of your time working, you should be enjoying it (Eccl. 5:18–19). God says He will give you the desires of your heart, and if working in a particular field is your desire, He is willing to grant you that blessing. The highlight about working at what you love is that it brings out the best in you and glorifies God. You may often shrug off your desires as being fickle, yet those very desires may be God's will for you. Moses desired to help his fellow Israelites, but went about it the wrong way. Then forty years later God called him to go back and deliver his brothers from slavery. You may desire to do something bigger than you, and you may have even tried to do it and failed. Keep seeking God and keep trying — your dream will happen in due course.

Examine Your Life

If you have done your best to honor God in your work but are unhappy with the work you are doing, it's time to examine your life. So what is bothering you about your work? Did you take the first work opportunity to arise, or did you prayerfully consider it before entering into that career or business choice? Do you need a career change? Have you constantly thought about doing something but lacked the courage to undertake it? Maybe you've thought of going back to school to improve your skills or start something new. Whatever it is, you need to either renew your mind-set about your work or change the work to the kind you love.

Find Your Calling

Considering that you spend more time working than doing any other activity, it would be beneficial to you and those you serve through your work to find and do the work you like. In other words, do the work that is your calling. Why? To reach your full potential in life or fulfill your destiny, which is all wrapped up in the work you do, you need to learn what your calling is.

To know your calling is to know what you're gifted at doing. Your calling is what you dream. What is your vision or dream? If you are unsure what your calling is, consider this: The secret to finding your purpose is to identify what you enjoy doing so much that you would be willing to do it for free. Then develop yourself in that area and become really good at it so people are willing to pay you to do it. You will find that the thing you love doing the most, the thing that gets you all excited (while it doesn't excite others), is where your calling lies. Knowing your purpose and living it out may not come overnight. For any dream to become a reality, you will need to work steadily at it (Eccl. 5:3). In working toward your dream, you may have put much effort into things you are not destined for and may have failed. But don't give up. Success is often several trials and failures away. You should use any failure to propel you forward to try something new. Trying something new or reworking something you've tried before just might lead to the fulfillment of your dream and bring you great joy.

Seek God

Furthermore, if you want to know your purpose, you must know God and seek Him. It is God who created you, and no one knows you like He does. He knows exactly who you are, why you were born at this time, what resources you have available to you, and who you love. Since He created you and knows details about your life you don't know yet, He's the best source to go to for direction. He created you on purpose with a purpose; to find out what that is, ask Him.

Consider seeking God concerning the desire in your heart and determine from Him what you need to do to accomplish it. I have a friend who had a great career in the hospitality industry, yet he had a desire in his heart to open a business in a completely different industry. Doing this seemed illogical, since he was already settled in his career. Furthermore, he had a family to consider. Yet the desire did not go away, and he sought God about what he should do. God gave him the direction he needed and through a minister confirmed that the desire of his heart was not against the will of God and that he should go full speed ahead to start this new business. That was the green light from God he had been waiting for. He went ahead in this new venture and today is happily enjoying a flourishing business. He still has the opportunity to work in the hospitality industry whenever possible.

Benefits of Loving Your Work

Why do I encourage you to know your calling? When you know your calling, are living the life you're destined to, or are doing the work you've been born to do, you'll be blessed. Doing what you love has its benefits. When you love your work, you will have the following:

* More energy you need to complete your work;

* Inner peace about what you're doing (you won't be miserable at work);

* The staying power to keep going: when others quit, you won't;

* The ability to face challenges undauntedly: obstacles

will be like stepping stones to you;

* Fulfillment from what you're doing because work will not be drudgery to you;

* Increased creativity: new ideas will easily spring to your mind;

* The freedom to create wealth

When you love the work you do you will not only create wealth but also enjoy a more productive and happy life.

Create Wealth Tip

Consider God your chief executive officer. You cannot be successful in any area of life without God. Whether you are an employee, a self-employed worker, or a business owner, you need God's hand on your work. While leading the children of Israel, Moses told God that he couldn't succeed in taking them to the Promised Land without God's presence (Ex. 33:15–16). God encouraged Joshua to continue the work Moses had started and led the children of Israel to possess their inheritance. However, God reiterated to Joshua the need to know Him—by speaking, meditating on, and living out His Word in his life. This was the only way to guarantee success in his work (Josh. 1:7–9). David did the work of a warrior—he was constantly in battle—yet he never made a move without hearing from God. Each time he followed God's instructions, he was successful. Let God be the CEO of your life—your work, career, business—in whatever you undertake to do, and you shall have good success.

CHAPTER 4

Tithe:
Pay Him First

To tithe or not to tithe—that is the question. Some think this Old Testament way is not relevant to us today. This argument comes down to unwillingness to give and to fear that enough won't be left over. Furthermore, if we were to follow the example of giving as the early church did, we would sell our possessions and give all the funds to the work of the Lord. So it's easier to start by giving that first 10 percent to God.

They said, Caesar's. Then He said to them, Pay therefore to Caesar the things that are due to Caesar, and pay to God the things that are due to God.

—Matthew 22:21 (AMP)

The first check you write belongs to God and no one else, not even the creditor.

—Larry Burkett, Crown Ministries

TOO FEW TITHE

W hy has the tithe become such a big issue in the church? Tithing is one of the most controversial topics—if not the most controversial topic—in Christianity. Having any form of discussion about tithing is almost a taboo for some. If you think talking about how much money you make is outrageous, delving into the subject of tithing is considered an even worse topic of discussion. The topic of tithing makes the majority of the membership at any church gathering cringe or get annoyed with their pastor for speaking about tithing. Little do most of them realize that being encouraged to pay the tithe and give offerings tremendously benefits those who do so faithfully.

So much has been written about tithing—for and against—that at first I was unsure about what I should and can say about this topic. I can say one thing for sure—over the past twenty seven years of serving God and bringing my tithe into the storehouse, I have never begged for bread. God has been faithful and protected me from destruction – financially and otherwise. I know that God honors us and blesses us as we give to His work for evangelizing, doing missions work, and edifying the body of Christ. When we tithe, many miracles come on account of obeying God's Word. A dear friend of mine can attest to the benefits and blessings of tithing. Here is what she says about tithing:

THE MIRACLE OF TITHING

During the period of December 2006 to October 2007, I experienced financial hardship. Things were so hard that I couldn't pay my rent in full at the end of the month; I had to pay it by installments. I received warning letters from the management of the apartment complex. Also I hardly had any spending money, and sometimes some of my bills were left unpaid. I literally lived from paycheck to paycheck, sometimes calling on my family for financial assistance.

One Saturday morning I was attending leadership classes, which were being held at church. On arrival I met one of the pastors and chatted for a while. The conversation that followed after greeting each other was God's way of revealing to me what was missing in my life and what I needed to do to open financial doors. I opened up my heart to this pastor and told him how difficult things were financially. He directly asked whether I paid my tithe. I told him that I did when I could afford it. As a caring pastor, he empathized with me, knowing that it can be scary at times to put God first in your finances by paying the tithe when money is limited. But he encouraged me to pay my tithe and watch God work in my life.

I took the pastor's advice, and from my next paycheck I started to pay my tithes. From that day my life changed. The Lord started to send persons into my life to bless me in various ways. When I was laid off of my job two weeks earlier than expected and didn't have enough money to pay my rent, the Lord placed a burden upon one of his daughter's hearts to bless me with enough money to pay my rent, my tithes, my telephone bill, and to purchase my transit pass for the month. I even had some left over for spending as I pleased.

Shortly after this, the floodgates of heaven literally opened, and blessings were poured out so much that I didn't have room enough for them. I lived in my apartment for about a year and five months with only a broken bed in the bedroom, two folding chairs, a centre table, and two side tables in the living room. During one of my prayer times, I asked the Lord to provide a couch so that I could have weekly small group meetings in my home. A few days later I was speaking with a close friend about my desire to have small group meetings. I told her that I had not started and was not eager to because I had only two chairs. Her response was: "Why didn't you tell me? I have a set of chairs in my basement. Do you want them? They are good; you only have to clean them a bit. I also have an entertainment centre, a big TV, a stereo, a centre table with two side tables, and a complete bedroom set. You can have all of this. Arrange transportation and let me know when you are coming for it, OK?" "WOW!" was my response with tears in my eyes. The Lord had answered my prayer and added lots more. When I collected the furniture, I literally did not have enough room for all of the pieces. There were some extra pieces, and I was able to be a blessing to someone else. The Lord again blessed me by furnishing my home without any cash leaving my hands! To God be the glory.

One Sunday morning I wrote a cheque for fifty dollars and placed it in the offering plate. At end of the service a friend handed me a sealed envelope. When I arrived home and opened it, to my surprise it was a cheque for fifty dollars. In February 2008, the Lord blessed me with my first permanent, full-time job after working part time through agencies for seven years. Then in August, He blessed me with a better job— permanent, full-time, with great benefits. The position was a newly created position in the organization, just for me.

I can go on and on to list the many blessings the Lord bestowed on me after I was obedient to His Word and began paying my tithes. God is not a man that He should lie, nor the son of man that He should repent. Once He said it, He will do it. He said when we bring the tithe to his storehouse, He will bless us. The only thing you have to do is obey. I thank God for all that He had done (where He has brought me from), is still doing, and will continue to do in my life. Blessed be the name of the Lord!

WHY TITHE? THE BLESSING OF TITHING

What an awesome testimony of God's goodness. When we obey His Word, He will by all mean bless us. Our faith moves to great heights when we trust God in the midst of trouble; then we see Him come through for us. Praise God! Let's look more into why we should tithe.

The Tithe is your Covenant with God

Even before the establishment of the Law, men gave a tithe to the Lord. When he had defeated Chedorlaomer and the kings, Abram gave a tithe of the spoils from the war to the priest Melchizedek (Gen. 14:18–20). After this, God appeared to Abram a second time to confirm that he would be the father of many nations. On the run from his brother, Esau, and recognizing that he had met with God, Jacob vowed to give God a tenth of all God had given to him (Gen. 28:22).

When you tithe, consider that you are keeping a covenant with the One who is the source of all your blessings. Tithing will help you recognize that God, the Most High, is the source of all you have and will ever need.

The Tithe Is Holy to the Lord

> *"Thus all the tithe of the land, of the seed of the land or of the fruit of the tree, is the Lord's; it is holy to the Lord"*

—Lev. 27:30 (NASB).

God reverences the tithe you put into His storehouse. He honors it. When something is considered holy, God consecrates it or sets it apart for special use. Indeed, when you pay your tithe, it is not just money but money with a godly assignment attached to it. Paying the tithe is not to be taken lightly. When you miss paying your tithe, you hinder the work of the Lord because that tithe has a special assignment. It cannot be properly fulfilled because the money is unavailable.

The Tithe Blesses You and Protects You

> *"Will a man rob God? Yet you have robbed Me! But you say, 'In what way have we robbed You?' In tithes and offerings. You are cursed with a curse, for you have robbed Me, even this whole nation. Bring all the tithes into the storehouse, that there may be food in My house, and try Me now in this," says the Lord of hosts, "If I will not open for you the windows of heaven and pour out for you such blessing that there will not be room enough to receive it. And I will rebuke the devourer for your sakes, so that he will not destroy the fruit of your ground, nor shall the vine fail to bear fruit for you in the field," says the Lord of hosts; "And all the nations will call you blessed, for you will be a delightful land," says the Lord of hosts.*

—Malachi 3:8–12

This Scripture gives two choices: to tithe or not to tithe or to be blessed abundantly or to be cursed. God presents a challenge to you to test Him regarding the tithe. This is one area in which you can put God on trial to determine if His word is true. Is God really going to bless you so much that you would not be able to receive it all? When you tithe, you can examine your life to see if God has blessed you to overflowing. Not only that, but He promises to destroy the works of the Enemy against your finances. The fruit of the ground represents your work and finances. God will ensure that your work never fails, but that all you do will prosper and bring increase to you. The tithe is so personal. The tithe opens heaven's doors for you. The tithe propels God to reprimand the Enemy for you—ensuring that he does not come near to destroy your blessings. The tithe will cause all you do to succeed and not to fail. The blessing of the tithe will cause others to call you blessed. What a blessing the tithe can be to you.

The Tithe Keeps the Spirit of Mammon from Controlling You

Money is a master. It can rule you, or you can rule it. One way to keep money from having its grip on you is by tithing (Matt. 6:24). When you tithe, you put God first; He, not money, is the Master over your life.

Wrestling yourself from the clutches of money takes grace. Zacchaeus was a man controlled by money—he stole from others, taking more than what was required. When he met Jesus, however, the Spirit of God convicted him, and he was willing to give back four times what he had stolen. This act of repentance brought salvation to him and his household. This act of repentance truly made him a son of Abraham, a child of God (Luke 19:1–9).

On the other hand, another man—though, like many of us, he was considered religious in that day—was held captive by the spirit of mammon. When Jesus told him to sell all he had and give to the poor, he was clearly saddened that Jesus would ask him to do such a thing. He was willing to keep what he had rather than have eternal life (Matt. 19:16–24). This is the plight not only of the rich, but of any believer who allows money to control him or her. When you are able to give away what you have, you are in control of it. Don't allow money to control you.

VIEW THE TITHE FROM THIS PERSPECTIVE

If you search the Scriptures, you will find other reasons for tithing, but surely some will say they have heard it all and are still unconvinced. But what if you look at the tithe from another perspective? See your tithe from this viewpoint:

1. As a "seek first the kingdom of God" practice. The first check from your income should go to God and God alone, not to the creditor or yourself. If you put God first in your money affairs, He will add to your life all you need and desire.

2. As giving back to God what is rightfully His. God could have demanded all you make; after all, it is all His. However, He requested only 10 percent of your gross income because He knows you need to take care of the needs of you and your family. I have noticed that no matter how tight things were in the past, whatever was left was enough to take care of me and my family. Whenever extra was needed, God always made a way—or sometimes I realized I didn't need the extra after all.

3. As a yoke breaker. Faithfully paying the tithe will destroy the spirit of consumerism and selfishness so many hoard in their hearts. It will break mind-sets such as, "I've got to have it all. It's my money, and I can do whatever I want with it; after all, I worked hard for it." When you don't tithe, you allow the spirit of greed to hover over your life; greed can destroy your soul. What benefit is it to you if you gain many possessions but lose your soul?

4. As a memorial you place before the Lord that will save you and your family. Look at Cornelius in the book of Acts; he had not yet heard the gospel, but the Bible makes special mention of his giving being like a memorial before God. That giving provoked God to send Peter to share the good news with him and his family so all could be saved. Furthermore, he was the first Gentile to hear the gospel. Recognize this: God pays special attention to your tithing and giving. To give or faithfully tithe, even in the midst of economic turmoil, can provoke God to do great

things for you. Have you ever wondered if that missing dream in your life could be fulfilled or if that prevailing problem could be solved, if only you gave to God what belongs to Him—the tithe?

5. As a form of worship to God, an indication that you honor God. The Lord said in His Word that the priest robbed Him by not paying his tithes and offerings. In other words, God was deprived of the tithe and offering that were rightfully and legally due to Him. This, of course, dishonors God and in no way shows that you reverence Him. When you tithe or give to Him what is rightfully His, however, you offer a sacrifice of praise, an emblem of worship. When you tithe, you also say thank you to Him.

6. As a way to keep things in perspective. Paying the tithe reminds you that God is your source, the supplier of all your needs. God puts a challenge before us. "'And try Me now in this,' says the Lord of hosts, 'If I will not open for you the windows of heaven and pour out for you such blessing that there will not be room enough to receive it'" (Mal. 3:10). Have you challenged God by bringing your tithe into His storehouse?

7. As a destroyer. The tithe halts the work of the Enemy in your life. God's Word is clear that when you rob Him, you are cursed. How many troubles do you have in your life? How do your finances measure up? Are you beyond struggling to make ends meet? Have you considered that maybe your problems are

the result of a self-imposed curse? Have you failed to honor God's Word and align your finances to His will by faithfully paying the tithe and giving your offering? When God rebukes the devourer for your sake (Mal. 3:11), this is not just about blessing you financially but about blessing your whole life. Consider the tithe.

8. As a means through which you become a blessing. The tithe is the road to receiving blessings and to being a blessing. When you release the money you call 'your money' into the kingdom of God as a tithe, it attracts God's blessings to you. As a result, people will call you 'blessed'. You don't need to say, "I am blessed," because people will see this without you saying it! People will see that you are blessed because of your generosity and your godly life. People will call you blessed because you will become a blessing to them through the tithe and offering you bring to the Lord. The Lord said the tithe is needed so there may be meat in His storehouse; that meat is disbursed to others through evangelism and missions. That meat is intended to help the people of God and those who need salvation both physically and spiritually.

9. As a beautifier. The tithe will cause God to make you a delightful person. You will possess joy and peace in your soul, even when the going gets tough. You will be pleasing not only to God but also to those around you (Mal. 3:12).

10. As an act of obedience to God's command. "Bring all the tithe" is a command and not optional. God requires it. If you desire to obey God in all things, then in this you must also yield your will to Him and do what He instructs you to do. Remember, God always instructs for your benefit, as any loving father does. God set apart the tithe for your good. You just need to trust and obey.

11. As a poverty breaker. The tithe destroys the spirit of poverty. If you are not blessed, you are cursed. If you do not have abundance, you have lack or poverty. Logically speaking, when you pay out money, you have less than before, yet God says when you pay the tithe, you will end up with more. God's Word defies logic; His thoughts are far above ours. The world will tell you to hold onto your money because God does not need it. But the world's logic is skewed and thinks only of itself. "Honor the Lord from your wealth and from the first of all your produce; so your barns will be filled with plenty and your vats will overflow with new wine" (Prov. 3:9–10 NASB). When you honor God with your tithe, you are guaranteed that you will have all you need. God's logic says that when you tithe and give, you will have more. Trust God's logic, tithe, and He will break the spirit of poverty from your life.

TRUST GOD AND RETURN THE TITHE

We established earlier in this book that God is the source of all we have, all we need now, and all we will need for the future. The only source of the money we receive and possess is God, the ultimate source. All those things— our time, talents, ideas, knowledge, strength, and possessions—God gave us. So when God says to return the tithe, He's not asking much of us at all. When we return the tithe, we are saying, "Thank You" to the source of it all. We're not just returning money to God but returning in part our thanks for good health, education, talents, gifting, creativity, our homes, and more.

God is the only source of what we have. From creation until now, God has provided for us. The psalmist says that this earth and all who live in it belong to God. So when God—who gave it all and owns it all— says to bring some back to His storehouse, how can we in our hearts say no? How can we say in our hearts, "This is my money, and I'll do whatever I want to with it?" God has given us not just the provision but the seed (our tithes and offerings) to keep the provision coming, but we reject it and then wonder why we're always lacking. We should return the tithe to the Lord. In doing so, we receive His blessing of 'meat in the storehouse'— to feed and bless us spiritually and in all areas of our lives.

Tithing Takes Faith

If for whatever reason you are afraid to tithe, feel the fear and do it anyway. Tithing takes courage—trusting God in spite of your insecurities. As you place that tithe in the storehouse, remember that God is your source and that He will take care of all your needs according to His riches in glory by Christ Jesus. Prove Him, and you will see God pour out His blessing on you over and above your expectations. You will, in turn, become a blessing to others.

CHAPTER 5

Save:
You're Next in Line (Bless Yourself)

Financial advisors teach that you should pay yourself first. Though the practice of saving is good, you should remove the negative thinking behind saving—that you should save for a rainy day or an emergency or in case you become unemployed. You should give the practice of saving a positive purpose. In other words, change the emphasis of savings from a negative perspective to a positive one. The habit of saving is a good one when you do it properly and for the right reasons.

Four things are small on the earth, but they are exceedingly wise: The ants are not a strong people, but they prepare their food in the summer.

—Proverbs 30:24–25 (NASB)

The "spending" habit must be replaced by the "saving habit" by all who attain financial independence.

—Napoleon Hill, The Laws of Success

THE PREVAILING HABIT OF NOT SAVING

In North America a compelling fact noted since 2007 is that the national savings rate fell below zero since the Great Depression. The average household carries high credit card debt and little or no savings. The financial crisis has provided evidence of this non-saving trend. This negative savings rate and high-debt ratio of today's North American households has resulted in the repossession of many homes, and the debt crisis has scattered and devastated many families. The problem we face is one that falls on our shoulders. We have become a society of consumers who want everything instantly and are willing to go into debt because of it. Needless to say, financial institutions have easily satisfied consumer demands and are more than ready to keep them in bondage.

Coupled with the lack of savings is the fact that many households live from paycheck to paycheck. For many too much month is left at the end of the money. In other words, after all the bills have been paid, nothing is left over to cover the living expenses for the rest of the month. People spend more money than they earn. As a result, households resort to credit cards as an easy means to cover the rest of the month. But sadly, as easy as access to funds may seem, the result is a negative spiral of debt that seems to have no end.

As for having a reserve fund (an emergency fund, as financial advisors call it), very few have enough saved to cover at least three months of living expenses. Whether we like it or not, unexpected events such as car repairs, household repairs, or a loss of income for a period of time do occur. Many families in Canada and United States struggle with high debt loads against modest savings and often insecure income flow. They have a high debt-service ratio over 40%, and are faced with rising interest rates, consumer prices and high job loss.

So where do you fall in? Are you a saver or non-saver? If you are not saving or not saving as you would like, what are some of the challenges you face? Do you work but your income doesn't even cover the ever increasing cost of living? Do you feel you have to use credit cards to cover some of your living expenses? Maybe you're able to pay all your bills but there is hardly anything is left over to save. As for retirement, maybe you've already concluded that you won't have one. You think you will have to work all the days of your life to make ends meet. The credit card statement keeps coming, and no matter how much you try to cut it down, the balance doesn't seem to get any smaller. The mortgage is too high, and you wish that maybe you'd taken a smaller house. Sometimes you are close to missing one of the payments. The constant debt seems endless, and saving anything for the future seems highly unlikely. If any of this describes you, that's understandable. However, to get out of the clutches of debt, build a future for yourself and your family, and discover financial independence, you need to develop the habit of saving.

WHY SHOULD WE SAVE?

Some say there's no point to saving. Considering the recent financial crisis, from which many have lost property and their life's savings, many are disheartened. In addition, the saving process seems like a long, slow journey without reward. We will take a look at both biblical and practical reasons why saving is necessary.

Save to Give Yourself Your Own Paycheck

Ponder this: You wake up early each day to prepare for work, probably two hours ahead of time or more. Your day at work is at least eight hours, and your commute is at least two. For some, the time dedicated to work is more than twelve hours. After working so hard, how much of the money you earn do you pay to yourself? Seriously, you spend the majority of your waking hours for someone else. Have you ever considered that you should pay yourself? Saving is like paying yourself. After paying your tithe and taxes, which are taken out before you see your paycheck, you should at least pay yourself the equivalent of one hour of each day you've worked.

On average that one hour works out to be approximately 12 percent of your gross income. Consider giving yourself a paycheck before you pay the creditors.

Saving Will Help You Kick
the Habit of Spending

I know some think that the way to reward themselves when they receive their paycheck is to spend some of it. Unfortunately, they often spend all of it or more than they have. Making savings our second money step whenever we receive an increase will help curb our habit of spending more than is necessary.

In financial circles you are advised to pay yourself first, but in Christian circles you are advised to pay the Lord first, then yourself. You become second in line if you put your money into registered and tax-deductible retirement accounts. Registered savings accounts help to reduce the effect of taxes paid from your gross pay, a benefit you will enjoy when you prepare your annual income tax return and during your retirement years.

Save for You and Your Family's Future

Look at your job from a different perspective. You are working not for some stranger, but for your family. The people you are working for are waiting at home. As you wake each day and go to work, remind yourself why you are going to work. Furthermore, the income you make is not only for immediate family needs but also for their future. Earning an income is commendable, but it doesn't stop at taking care of immediate needs. You have a responsibility to provide for your family's future needs. The plan to make money but not save some of it is incomplete. If you fail to save, you fail to provide for your family. First Timothy 5:8 says, "But if anyone does not provide for his own, and especially for those of his household, he has denied the faith and is worse than an unbeliever" (NASB). As harsh as it may sound, we are like unbelievers if we do not fully live up to our responsibility to our families and God. In the kingdom of God, you must not only grow in spiritual things but also mature in your daily life. Therefore, make saving part of your life for the benefit of you and your family.

Save for the Unexpected

The wise one tells us to consider the ways of the ant. "Go to the ant, you sluggard! Consider her ways and be wise, which, having no captain, overseer or ruler, provides her supplies in the summer, and gathers her food in the harvest" (Prov. 6:6–8). Just like nature, our lives operate according to seasons. Because we don't always live in excess or abundance, we need to be like the ant. The ant works steadily in the season when conditions are good and stores up when the harvest is plentiful. The ant is fully aware that seasons will change and that going to work and gathering will not always be feasible. Therefore, he prepares for low periods when supplies are limited.

We ought to be like the ant. Instead of using extra

income to buy what we don't need, we should save. Dry seasons come when savings are needed to act as a buffer. Seasons may include times of illness or times when our income streams may be cut off or be less than expected. We need to prepare for such contingencies. As much as we would not like these things to happen, they do happen in this fallen world—and usually when we least expect it. If we habitually set aside a portion of our income, however, unexpected events that require additional cash flow will not catch us off guard.

Save for a Good Reason

Paul admonished the Corinthian church to save weekly so they would be able to give toward the work of the ministry. "On the first day of every week each one of you is to put aside and save, as he may prosper, so that no collections be made when I come" (1 Cor. 16:2 NASB). Nothing is wrong with that at all. So many good reasons abound for saving to give toward missions, hospitals, Christian universities, or your church building fund. We may even save for a much-needed family holiday. Yes, God richly gives us all things to enjoy (1 Tim. 6:17), and a good rest can revive our whole being. We can also save so we are prepared to invest in opportunities, such as buying a franchise or existing business. We can also use the cash flow toward developing your business if you're a business owner, purchasing real estate, funding our children's education, or blessing our child with a down payment on his or her new home. The point is, saving brings freedom and gives us the ability to bless ourselves, our loved ones, and others.

Save and Make Ready for New Opportunities

Having ready cash can be a good thing. Often investment opportunities come our way that we would consider, but we lack even the first cent to make the investment. Limited cash hinders opportunities available to us. When cash is in hand, we can now go beyond the investigation stage if we have concluded that the venture would be a good one.

Maybe you have been presented with business opportunities and have felt the frustration and embarrassment of not being able to move ahead with them. Having savings can help you step into new and exciting opportunities. When financial institutions see that you have the habit of saving on a regular basis, you show that you are financially sound and can be trusted with their funds. Should you need a loan to invest in an appreciable asset or investment, financial institutions will generally be more willing to lend to you as opposed to someone who has high credit card debt and lacks any savings.

Saving Can Help You Broaden Your Horizons

Have you ever wanted to upgrade your level of education, start a course based on your personal interest, or provide for your children's higher education? If you are a habitual saver, you can allocate a portion of your savings toward education. In Canada, the registered education savings plan provides an opportunity for parents to invest in their children's education with the government's financial backing of 20 percent for every dollar invested up to four thousand dollars. Unfortunately, this is an opportunity many miss because they are not habitual savers. Some children must work while studying to make their way through the university because their parents weren't forward thinking. Other children do not bother pursuing this level of education because the cost is too high, an obstacle that seems too great for them. Your children may lose the opportunity to better themselves if you do not save now. When you save, you invest in your children's future.

GIVE YOUR SAVINGS A POSITIVE ASSIGNMENT

I know I mentioned this earlier in the chapter, but reiterating the need to give your savings a positive assignment is important. In financial circles, you are encouraged to save and, more specifically, to always have an emergency fund of three to six months' living expenses. Though this may appear to be good advice, it can have a negative effect on how you view your finances. Have you ever noticed that the moment your emergency fund reaches a desired level, an emergency arises, and you must use that money? What about that living expenses fund—as soon as you have it, you're out of a job. Why? Your savings carried out the assignment you gave to it. If you approach your money from this view—saving for a rainy day—a rainy day will certainly come! Please don't misunderstand me. Sure, setbacks and problems arise, but inviting problems with a negative approach to your savings doesn't help.

When my husband and I set a goal to purchase a house, we saved toward it, and for sure we got that house. When we passed through some challenging times, my mind-set changed. I had no particular assignment for my savings, and sometimes I didn't save.

This is the mistake most people make at some point in time—they fail to keep setting financial goals and giving their savings a positive purpose. Why? They become overwhelmed with the financial responsibilities of paying a mortgage, maintaining a home, keeping their jobs, and focusing more on the present issues of living rather than on preparing for the future.

When I did save, it was for the wrong reasons—for that rainy day or just in case of an emergency. I didn't think I should save to bless myself or to use my savings for investment purposes. Then month after month I saw my savings dwindle. Why? I didn't have any specific assignment for saving—not even for the golden years. Also since my purpose was for rainy days, rainy days seemed to come quite often.

Successful and rich people save not from the perspective that they will lose their jobs or that their businesses will collapse; they save for purposes of investment—to be ready for the next great opportunity that comes their way. Any successful person I have encountered or read about saves with a positive purpose in mind. Frankly, such people are always looking for new opportunities. They do not think they will lose a job and therefore need to save in case of emergency or business failure. Their thinking is structured around being successful, and they save with that in mind. On the other hand, the mind-set of a poor man or one with a poverty mentality is that he must save in case something goes wrong. If he thinks that way, that rainy day will come for sure.

Do you understand what I'm saying? Your thoughts affect your money. Think about it. Look at my personal story above to get your mind thinking about how you have approached saving money.

A FEW FUN SAVING TIPS

Refuse to give your savings a negative assignment such as 'saving for a rainy day' or 'having an emergency fund'. Maybe you can call it an 'Opportunity Fund.' Give purpose to it. Consider giving your savings an assignment. Name every savings fund or savings bottle (if you like that method). For example, 'Special Giving' (like birthdays, missions), 'Vacation Fund,' 'Education Fund,' 'Investment Fund,' 'Freedom Fund,' 'Findependence Fund/Registered Savings Account.' The names will help remind you what you are saving that money for.

Decide How Much You Will Save

Apart from giving purpose to your savings by naming each fund appropriately, set a main savings goal. You may tell yourself, This year I will bless myself with 20 percent from all the income I receive. Once you determine the amount, which may be only an estimate, determine how much you will allocate to each savings fund you have. You don't need to have separate accounts for each, but just knowing how much is assigned to each savings fund gives you a clear vision of where you are going. You can keep a spreadsheet or some other type of record using personal finance software to track your progress. It is exhilarating when you see yourself getting closer and closer to your goals.

Just Save What You Can

Don't worry if you lack a three- to six-month quota that a financial planner would advise you to have. Your job is to start saving on a consistent basis (weekly, biweekly, monthly) no matter how small that amount may be. Your savings will grow as you gradually build it. You can help your savings habit to increase by setting up automatic withdrawals from your main account to your savings account, but you can save other ways too. I have a friend who takes the two-dollar bills she receives and puts them in a container. When she takes a vacation, she uses what she accumulated in that box to either pay for her trip or use as spending money during her vacation. As a family, we have a huge bottle that we all place coins into as a way of helping our daughter learn to save. You may give a different purpose to it, but the exercise of physically putting that money away helps to form the habit in you.

Teach Your Children to Save

We live in a consumer-driven society, and businesses do all they can to induce even our children to spend. Our responsibility is to teach our children to form the habit of saving money from an early age. We shouldn't give our children everything. If we teach our children to tithe, save, give, and spend carefully from an early age, this practice will prove beneficial to us and our children in later years. From the time our children can understand what we say, we should start teaching good and sound financial principles based on God's Word.

Keep Covered While You Save

Unfortunately, many lack any life insurance. If they have a policy, it is insufficient to cover the needs of their family. The excuse of many is that we don't need to cover such risk. We are children of God, and He will take care of us. It may be true that God will take care of us, but do we know when our time on this earth is up?

Dedicate a portion of your savings account toward payments of your insurance premium. You should possess enough life insurance coverage to provide not only funeral expenses but also your family's ongoing needs. Life insurance is like having an instant estate to leave as an inheritance for your children's children, especially if you don't have a reasonable amount saved and invested. If you systematically save, you are sure to become financially free.

CAUTION! DON'T GET LOST IN GATHERING

Though we should save, we shouldn't get attached to the money. We all know money is temporal. Many have worked hard for money only to see it quickly lost before their eyes. Saving or storing up possessions, if not done correctly, can cause us to miss heaven. In the parable of the rich man, the rich man stored up his excess; his focus was on relaxing, eating, drinking, and being merry (Luke 12:16–21). Isn't that what this world system tells us to do when we have more than enough or when we make it big? But that motive is out of alignment with God's will. God called this man a fool!

God's will is not for us to have all we can and sit on it and gloat over it. If we focus on all we have, like this man did, we will fail in our walk with God and miss heaven. The young ruler who went to Jesus, asking what he should do to make it to heaven, had the same problem as the rich man, who kept storing up his possessions. He obeyed the law and did all the right things, like Christians do, but still he missed the mark. When Jesus told him to sell all he had and give it to the poor so he would have treasure in heaven he couldn't do it. Money, not God, was his master. Money had a grip on him that he couldn't be free from to serve Jesus.

Consider what Jesus said about this young man and anyone enslaved by the stronghold of money. "How hard it is for those who have riches to enter the kingdom of God!" (Mark 10:23). Then He said in Mark 10:24–25, "Children, how hard it is for those who trust in riches to enter the kingdom of God! It is easier for a camel to go through the eye of a needle than for a rich man to enter the kingdom of God" (emphasis added).

Make sure you are rich not only in money but also toward God. Saving your money or accumulating wealth with the wrong motive causes you to worship your money and possessions rather than God. You no longer depend on God because you think you have it all or have arrived. You have a sense of false security and think you're self-sufficient. You're not. Like Jesus said, one day your soul will be required of you (Luke 12:20). In other words, God will judge your heart, not your possessions. Also remember that all the possessions you gather here on this earth will stay here. So Jesus admonishes us to store up treasures in heaven because this one can be easily lost, stolen, or destroyed.

Simply put, attach eternal value to your money through giving and investing in the kingdom of God— that is part of laying up treasures in heaven. Also, as Solomon so clearly reminded us, when you die, someone else will take over all you now possess. So you have no need to guard your possessions. You should rather build treasure in heaven—let your life and money do the work of the Lord. Don't be like the rich man or young ruler. View savings in its proper perspective.

GOD PROVIDES YOUR SAVINGS TOO

I have found that Scripture offers little discussion on the topic of saving. Why is this so? Simply because God promises to take care of us. God promises us His blessings; He promises to prosper us as we obey His Word. Since God delights in the prosperity of His children and constantly reiterates this in His Word, we should not worry. Yet as responsible citizens of the kingdom, God expects us to save for our benefit, our family, and others. God, our omnipresent provider, is never limited in His resources and can bless us anytime. This great God never lacks and never needs to store up. He has promised us that as we seek His kingdom and its righteousness first, all we need, including our savings, will be provided for us.

Saving Frees You

Saving helps relieve you of worry about the unexpected. Also, many view the habit of saving as one of the attributes of a successful person. See yourself succeeding and progressing every time you save. Pay yourself for your hard work. Every time you save, thank God and ask Him to bless and increase your savings.

CHAPTER 6

Invest:
Let Money Work for You

This may seem like a scary topic given the recent chaos in the financial markets, but you should still make investments—and good ones. Truth be told, though investing is not an easy-as-pie task, it is doable with God's direction and the help of a sound financial professional.

For to everyone who has, more shall be given, and he will have an abundance; but from the one who does not have, even what he does have shall be taken away.

—Matthew 25:29 (NASB)

Divide your portion to seven, or even to eight, for you do not know what misfortune may occur on the earth.

—Ecclesiastes 11:2 (NASB)

The realities of life daily remind us that we are getting older and, as such, will be faced with physical limitations. We know that one day we will be unable to fully exert our strength or have full strength to make money. It is prudent for every man and woman to begin right now to find ways to make money work for them. In other words, all of us need to think ahead and prepare for our future and that of our children and their children. If we have money working for us and make wise investments, what we gain can be beneficial to us, our loved ones, and others.

But investing seems like a big challenge for some. Many think that investing involves large sums of money; therefore, it is out of their reach. Others are fearful of putting their money 'out there' because they don't want to lose it. The reasons for not investing can be many, but to be fruitful in every aspect of our lives, we will need to consider making good investments. Let's examine why some choose not to make investments part of their financial plan.

WHY YOUR MONEY ISN'T WORKING FOR YOU

The Markets Can Be Scary

Over the past few years, many disasters have shaken the financial markets—major investment losses for high net worth individuals, losses of pension funds and other firms, a rise in the homeless rate because of foreclosures, a hike in jobless claims, the bankruptcy of top investment firms, criminal charges filed against those who have swindled money from others, and even the suicide of some who couldn't face others because of bad investment decisions. And the list goes on. No wonder investing appears to be a rather scary topic lately.

Still, we should make investments—and good ones. Needless to say, the stock market is like one huge maze in which we can become lost. The key, however, is focus—not on the entire market, but on specific areas or segments of it.

Over the years I have seen those who have been 'burned' by the market downfalls or have made losses due to bad investment decisions or lack of investment knowledge or advice. On the other hand, I have also witnessed firsthand, read about, or heard of those who have made it big by investing wisely. Even with the markets as they are today, many are still making good returns on their investments in the midst of the market turmoil. Though the area of personal finance can offer many ups and downs, the job is doable with God's direction and the help of a sound financial professional. We should seek wise counsel even if we are capable of making sound investment decisions; hiring an experienced financial professional to assist us in our investment strategy would be prudent.

You See the Stock Market as the Only Investment Avenue

Investments are not limited to the stock market. Even within the stock market different ways of investing can prove easier to understand and to invest in—mutual funds, exchange-traded funds, hedge funds (for the high net worth individual or corporation), segregated funds, fixed-income securities of various levels, and so forth. Other ways exist outside financial markets to make reasonable returns. These can include real estate (residential or commercial), business ventures, franchising, investing in gold or silver or antiques, reducing your mortgage, participating in a lending club and so on. With investing we are likely to make a substantially better return than with a savings account. However seek professional advise.

Whenever we think of investing, we shouldn't limit ourselves to the stock market. Other forms of investing can prove to be more beneficial.

Limited or No Savings? Then No Investing

Saving is the lowest level of investing—you make a very small return from your savings account. Having a savings account, however, is a good start. Unfortunately, if the habit of saving money is a challenge for you, or if you have no savings or only limited savings available, then investing will prove to be a challenge as well. So start at the beginning. Build your savings, then move up the financial ladder to investing. Be wise, even in saving, and research where you put your money—fees to withdraw or deposit, required days to hold funds before they are available to you, restrictions for bank machine withdrawals if you need funds urgently, and so on. Don't let small details become a surprise to you. Once you have built up your savings to a reasonable level, start investing some into an investment vehicle you or your financial advisor has researched and that you are comfortable with.

Lack of Investment Knowledge

Making excuses is very easy, and the excuse we make most often is that we don't know what to do or where to start. Of course, investing is a big topic, and even investment professionals tell us they are always learning. They will even acknowledge that all investment returns cannot be known; as such, maybe we should specialize in one area of the market more than any other.

As an investor, your job is to research and learn all you can about what you're interested in and to evaluate the risk and count the cost. In this financial world, seeking help is best. First, as a Christian investor, seek God, the One who knows all things. God admonishes you to ask for wisdom (James 1:5), God is pleased when you do and willing to give you the direction you need. Proverbs 3:5-6 commands you to involve God in all details of your life. Don't leave God out of whatever investment decisions you make. Remember, He knows all and is able to direct you in the right way. As you acknowledge Him in this area of your life, you should also get professional advice (Prov. 15:22). Safety and great help are available for those who seek wise counsel. Your investment plans are sure to succeed if you act on the wise counsel you receive.

Fear of Losing

The fear of losing what you have invested is very much part of the fear of failure. No one wants to lose his or her hard-earned money. Many would say it is harder to earn money than to lose it. That is true for many people, but not all. Few are able to lose it all and then gain more later. Your outlook and attitude determine whether you gain or lose money. Fear can hold you back and cause you to lose more by not investing. When you invest, it is not just about the money earned, but the experience gained. Even in cases of losses, you can learn from investing. To stay on the side of caution, however, either don't invest or don't invest all that you have if you cannot afford to lose it. Do your homework, research before investing, and seek professional advice so you can make an informed decision. Then move ahead and trust God, for He gives not the spirit of timidity but of a sound and balanced mind and of confidence that rests in Him and His ability.

WHY INVEST?

Money Attracts Money

One reality is that most who have wealth or enough to invest are generally not in need of more money, but they still make more money. This fact is in line with one of Jesus's parable. He said that those who have will receive more and that, for those who have little, what they have will be taken from them (Matt. 25:29). Money attracts money. Money that is well invested makes more money for the one who invests wisely. The disappointing part, however, is that most of those who make lots of money usually spend most of it on themselves. Money in the hands of the unrighteous is often wasted, but money in the hands of the righteous can do great things in the kingdom of God and for mankind. In the hand of the righteous, it can be distributed equitably to those in need.

Yes, as members of the body of Christ, we are distributors of wealth. We Christians should seek ways to invest and make money work on our behalf rather than just sit back and watch the unrighteous accumulate the majority of the wealth. Proverbs 13:22 tells us, "The wealth of the sinner is stored up for the righteous" (NASB), but Christians must be prepared to receive that wealth, which can start with investing.

To Leave an Inheritance

Investing can have eternal value if you leave an inheritance for your children and their children. As a good father or mother, you can show your love as well as God's love by leaving a legacy for your children. Giving an inheritance not only shows your love for them, but also teaches them that you thought of, planned for, and worked toward their future. As a righteous man or woman, the Bible says you will leave an inheritance for generations to come. Proverbs 13:22 says, "A good man leaves an inheritance to his children's children, but the wealth of the sinner is stored up for the righteous." Though I'm talking about finances, I believe that inheritance is also spiritual—it ensures that God is the central focus of their lives. As children of God, your children should continue to inherit the earth. How can they unless you leave them an inheritance, both physical and spiritual?

I know you might be saying to yourself that you don't have a lot to leave, but you can at least start off by having adequate insurance coverage. This can be a great help to your family when you pass from this earth to the blessed life with Jesus. It can also be the beginning of leaving an inheritance for your children. Often some see insurance as a "waste" or frown on it, thinking they should not be preparing for death too soon. But the fact of the matter is, unless Jesus comes before you die, you will leave this earth and pass onto the other side. So look at insurance as your instant estate. At least with adequate insurance, you can cover your final expenses and maintain the income level your family has come to depend on. Why should you leave your family worrying or stressing over your funeral expenses and debts when adequate insurance coverage would take care of those needs? Since you are a righteous man or woman, it is fitting to have proper insurance in place for the benefit of your spouse and children. This is a start to investing and leaving an inheritance for your children.

For Your Present and Future Needs

Although you are preparing for eternal life, you still need to do good here on this earth. The returns from investing can also help you and your family in your current lifestyle and later in life. How? You do not always need to work hard physically; increase can come if you put your money to work for you. Investing can also aid you in your golden years when you are not as young as you used to be—the reserve buildup from investing can maintain your lifestyle or standard of living.

To Bless Others and Promote the Kingdom Of God

If you look outside your immediate surroundings, you'll see that investing can help you help others. You can sometimes place your extra into church projects, missions, a hospital, a women's crisis center—no matter what, there is always a need. As God increases your investment portfolio, the profit is not only for you but for God's purposes as well. You can attach eternal value to what you're investing in by not setting aside all your increase for yourself, but by setting aside some of it for God. You can even will some of your estate to your church or a charitable organization that will use it wisely for the benefit of this hurting world. Whatever you do, set some of your portfolio aside to do something that honors God and promotes His kingdom and His love for this world. So investing is good, as you can see. Therefore, put your money to work—for yourself, for your generation, and for your God. Look at what you've been given and what you are able to do and start the investment process today.

GOD ENCOURAGES INVESTING

Cast your bread upon the waters, for you will find it after many days. Give a serving of seven, and also to eight, for you do not know what evil will be on the earth. If the clouds are full of rain, they empty themselves upon the earth; and if a tree falls to the south or to the north, in the place where the tree fails, there it shall lie. He who observes the wind will not sow, and he who regards the clouds will not reap. As you do not know what is the way of the wind, or how the bones grow in the womb of her who is with child, so you do not know the works of God who makes everything. In the morning sow your seed, and in the evening do not withhold your hand; for you do not know which will prosper, either this or that, or whether both alike will be good.

—Ecclesiastes 11:1–6

The Preacher in Ecclesiastes offers some great advice on investing. Investing is like casting your net out to sea—you have no guarantees. A fisherman will make either a great catch, a small one or receive nothing at all. The same goes with farming—you get either a great harvest or a not-so-great harvest. But neither the fisherman nor the farmer hesitates to do his business because his livelihood is at stake. If he doesn't act, then he won't know whether he could have done well.

When investing, you cast your bread—some of what you've earned—into the financial sea. You don't know what will work or what won't. But God says you should put your money to work and promises that you will find it many days later. In other words, you will make a return on your investment—not right away, but over time. Time is necessary for your money to work. Research has proven that over time, with all the ups and downs in the market, your money will make a better return over a longer period than over a shorter one. Investing is not an overnight event—it requires long-term commitment.

Additionally, investing requires diversification. In other words, you shouldn't keep all your investing eggs in one basket. The possibility exists that holding all your money in one fund, stock, or other investment vehicle could prove disastrous. If you keep all your eggs in one basket and it falls, you will have nothing to eat. The result would be a major loss should problems arise with that investment. Investing involves risk: the higher the return, the greater the risk and greater the probability of loss. Therefore, diversification is a strategy you can use to spread the risk across your portfolio. Within a diversified portfolio, some investments may perform well while others may incur losses. The gains and losses from each investment will create some balance and reduce the level of loss.

Though you are cautioned to diversify, because no investment is a sure thing, you shouldn't be timid about investing. Don't sit down and watch the wind and clouds. No farmer does that. Whether the weather is windy, cloudy, sunny, or rainy, the farmer does what he needs to—he plants, he tends his crops, and he harvests. Since he cannot predict what type of harvest he will have and which field will bring a better harvest, he plants and reaps regardless of weather conditions. From an investment perspective, if you keep thinking that general market conditions are unfavorable, you won't be likely to invest anything. As such you won't make any returns either.

The key is to put your money to work no matter what conditions are like. Just as a farmer needs faith to plant and believe he will make a harvest, you must have faith to invest and believe you will make a return on your investments. You are admonished not only not to be timid about investing but also to be busy about investing. Don't just invest occasionally; be diligent about it. The farmer is told to plant not only in the morning but also in the evening since he doesn't know what will prosper.

As an investor you should constantly be looking for and investing in new opportunities. The implication is that you must be diligent in investing. After you have considered all, counting the cost (Luke 14:28–30) and making an investment, look for another opportunity and work on it as well. Be diligent in the process of investing; making wise decisions takes hard work. Since you don't know what will work, spreading your investments well is best. In all you do, however, put God before you, and He will direct and prosper you.

INVESTING IS NOT FOR THE LAZY OR FEARFUL

For it is just like a man about to go on a journey, who called his own slaves and entrusted his possessions to them. To one he gave five talents, to another, two, and to another, one, each according to his own ability; and he went on his journey. Immediately the one who had received the five talents went and traded with them, and gained five more talents. In the same manner the one who had received the two talents gained two more. But he who received the one talent went away, and dug a hole in the ground and hid his master's money. Now after a long time the master of those slaves came and settled accounts with them. The one who had received the five talents came up and brought five more talents, saying, "Master, you entrusted five talents to me. See, I have gained five more talents." His master said to him, "Well done, good and faithful slave. You were faithful with a few things, I will put you in charge of many things; enter into the joy of your master." Also the one who had received the two talents

came up and said, "Master, you entrusted two talents to
me. See, I have gained two more talents." His master said
to him, "Well done, good and faithful slave. You were
faithful with a few things, I will put you in charge of many
things; enter into the joy of your master." And the one also
who had received the one talent came up and said,
"Master, I knew you to be a hard man, reaping where you
did not sow and gathering where you scattered no seed.
And I was afraid, and went away and hid your talent in
the ground. See, you have what is yours." But his master
answered and said to him, "You wicked, lazy slave, you
knew that I reap where I did not sow and gather where I
scattered no seed. Then you ought to have put my money
in the bank, and on my arrival I would have received my
money back with interest. Therefore take away the talent
from him, and give it to the one who has the ten talents."
For to everyone who has, more shall be given, and he will
have an abundance; but from the one who does not have,
even what he does have shall be taken away. Throw out
the worthless slave into the outer darkness; in that place
there will be weeping and gnashing of teeth.

—Matthew 25:14–30 (NASB)

This parable is used to explain many principles—that God has made us stewards over His wealth and how we should handle what has been entrusted to us. The Scripture also compares the faithful and diligent servant to the wicked and lazy one. We find something to learn in this teaching about investing God's way.

By grace, God appoints to each person the level of wealth, resources, and various blessings He knows each is capable of managing. As a wise God, Father, and Master, He is well able to determine what we can handle. Some will have more than others—and that's okay. We don't need to worry about or covet what the other person has. As children of God, we should simply acknowledge that our blessings are God given and that we should be thankful for what we have and where we are in life. Of course, where we are in life now is not the end—God has more in store for us.

But what kind of money manager are you? Are you fast acting and diligent or slow to act, lazy, and fearful? God has appointed to you some measure of blessings. What are you doing with them?

Two out of three men in the story went out and began doing business with the money they had been given. That immediate response to this business opportunity shows their positive attitude toward business. This fast action resulted in their being profitable. They made a positive return on their investments.

What about you? You have been blessed with some financial resources above what you need immediately. Are you putting that money to work to make more money? Upon his return the master rewarded these two action takers and gave them double what he had previously given to them to manage. Unless God sees you working diligently with what you have to invest and making profit from it, how will He know—and how will you know—that you can manage more responsibility?

The management of money is a big responsibility, as we have discussed throughout this book. God blesses us with more so we will be a blessing to others. Therefore, until we become good money managers of what we currently have, we shouldn't expect God to bring more our way. The greater the blessing, the greater the responsibility. With our go-getter attitude and willingness to diligently work at investing, we need to show God that we can eventually handle more responsibility.

Would God call you a lazy person? The third man in this story was called lazy and wicked. That seems like a hard judgment to make. After all, he didn't lose the money; he just kept is safe. Let's take a closer look at this man. He too acted immediately but not like the others. He searched out a safe place to hide the money and went to work burying it. Why did he do that? Was it because that was the best option? No. He hid the money out of fear and a lack of understanding. He had a misconception about his master—that he was hard or shrewd to work with. The master was a savvy businessperson who profited in places where he hadn't even made an initial investment. Since this man didn't understand that business or investing could be profitable in more ways than one, he lost heart and hid the money. His weak explanation regarding his failure to do anything with the money resulted in a hard judgment; the master called him lazy.

But we may say that he worked hard at keeping the master's money safe. A lazy person is not someone who does nothing at all but one who gives up along the way and accomplishes nothing (Prov. 12:27; 13:4). The master left money with them so they could make more money. He didn't intend for them to hide it. If this servant had at least put the money in the bank and collected interest, he would have done better than burying it.

What are you doing with the money in your hand? Have you buried it? Have you at least invested the money in a high-interest account or government-investment certificate? Investing takes hard work. The business of doing business, especially with someone else's money, requires diligence—sticking to the task—to make a good return. Whether investing in a business or a portfolio, you must be willing to go the long haul. This level of money management is not for the shortsighted, but for those who can look ahead and keep pressing forward, even in tough times.

The period between receiving the money from the master and the time he returned must have been filled with challenges along the way. At times, the servants may have suffered losses. Yet in the end they knew they were able to make a profit. An important key to successful investing is to stick to the task.

The judgment the master pronounced on this lazy servant has often troubled me. Why didn't the master let the servant keep the money? The lazy servant never took ownership of what the master gave him. He failed to see himself as a money manager. The faithful servants, however, recognized that the master entrusted them with the money and as such believed in their ability to manage it well. While the faithful servants took personal responsibility, the lazy servant kept thinking, This isn't my money, and I don't want to lose it. I'll just hide it and give it back to the owner when he comes. Do you realize that this lazy servant took a standoffish attitude toward the responsibility he was given? When the master returned, the servant said, "See, you have what is yours." Because of his fear of losing the money, he hid it. But since he never took ownership or responsibility of the money, he lost any chance of keeping it. The master took it away from him and gave it to someone else who already had it in abundance.

Do you find yourself in the same dilemma? Perhaps you have been blessed, but you're afraid to invest your money because you don't want to lose it. You don't want God to consider you a careless Christian who is wasteful of His resources. Have you ever considered that maybe God blessed you with excess so you could make more and therefore bless more people? Think about it. Have you even considered that God has given to you what He knows you are well able to manage? If you don't manage your money well, you will lose it. The growth of anything mismanaged ultimately diminishes, comes to an end, and will eventually be lost. Yes, the money you have is ultimately God's, but He has given it to you to properly manage while you are here on this earth. Don't be afraid. Step out in faith and trust God to help you invest and manage His resources well. Whatever concerns you concerns Him—even the business of investing.

The master's judgment on the lazy servant ended with these words: "For to everyone who has, more shall be given, and he will have an abundance; but from the one who does not have, even what he does have shall be taken away." That seems like a very unfair statement. The rich don't need more than what they have, yet this is the reality of life even today. Why would the rich get richer and the poor get poorer? The rich always see an opportunity and seize it. Look at the two faithful servants; the master gave them money, and they seized the opportunity to go out and make more. The rich look for ways they can serve others and solve problems and in the process are paid for providing services or products. The poor or those who lack, however, usually think of how they can keep what little they have, but they soon consume it by paying for the products or services the rich provide. The lazy servant in the story hid the money instead and probably would have spent it all if he hadn't.

Where are you in all this—getting richer or getting poorer? Are you like many poor ones who fail to see opportunities anywhere that would solve problems and, at the same time, be financially beneficial to them? Or do you constantly think of how to spend money or keep it safe instead of looking for ways to invest it? If you find yourself in the "getting poorer" categories, seek God for help because His desire is to see you on the "getting richer" side so you have the ability to give toward good works.

The bottom line is that God encourages you to do something, no matter how small it may seem, with what He has given to you. Whatever you do must be pleasing to God, but the objective is for you to do something with what you have been given.

You must take what God has given to you and invest it—money included. He gives you a little to see how you might handle it. As you can see from the story, if you work with what you are given, manage it well, and are profitable in it, God will bless you with more. On the other hand, if you sit on what you possess or poorly manage it, for sure you will lose it all. Scripture clearly states that the one who has little will lose it—it will be taken away from him or her. And to the one who has more, more will be given.

At first glance this response may seem unfair, but if you have a small amount of money and cannot manage it well, you will certainly lose it due to your own mismanagement. In your failure to do well with the small amount, someone wiser, more committed, more faithful, and more responsible than you will most likely take it from you. This is the result of embracing a poor mind-set, practicing poor money management skills, and being outwitted by others. If you are able to hone good money skills, however, you will see that increase comes because you have learned the ins and outs of doing business and working with money—you can determine how best to handle it. When God sees you develop these skills and become committed and remain faithful in the process, He will cause you to be profitable. Also as you faithfully tithe and willingly give from your blessing, He will make certain to increase the blessings on your life. Therefore, be faithful with what you have, invest it, and profit from it. Then watch as God blesses you with more!

INVESTING IS A BALANCING ACT

Like everything in life, we need to strike a balance. With investing we should take heed to some useful advice and words of caution.

Expect a Return on Your Investment

The Bible tells us that the expectation of the righteous will be satisfied (Prov. 23:17-18). The Lord is always ready to give us the desires of our hearts and whatever we ask of Him according to His will (Ps. 37:4; Jn. 16:23). Whatever we expect is what we will receive. As we discussed earlier, some people are fearful about investing. Some make investments, but few believe they will make a good return on their investments. We should approach investing with the conviction that God will prosper us in it. If we have the quality of a blessed man or woman, certainly we will prosper (Ps. 1:1–3).

Also, the more dollars we invest, the more dollars we expect to be returned to us. Simply put, if we invest one hundred dollars at a 10 percent return, we expect to receive ten dollars (using simple interest). If we invest one thousand dollars for the same 10 percent return, we will make one hundred dollars. Aim to invest as much as possible in profitable businesses.

Get Professional Help—Even a Christian Financial Advisor, If Possible

Employ the assistance of a qualified financial advisor, accountant, or other professional when making investment decisions. If you are able to hire a Christian financial advisor, you are likely to find someone who has similar values and will also give advice that is Bible based. Since a greater level of risk is involved in investing, careful research and skill are needed to make the appropriate investments based on your risk tolerance. Make sure you get the necessary help you need.

Think Long Term

Make investments that profit you not only in the now but in the future for your children. The investments you make should outlive you and be passed onto your children and their children.

If You Don't Understand the Investment Opportunity, Don't Invest

Err on the side of caution. Nothing in life is built successfully due to lack of knowledge, wisdom, or understanding. These three attributes are necessary to make any undertaking, including investing, successful (Prov. 24:3–4). As mentioned earlier, hire someone who is skilled in this area but don't be a blind investor. Learn from the advisor, read some books, read the investment section of the newspaper, or subscribe to a money magazine.

Know What You Have

Evaluate your portfolio at least annually. You should always know where you stand financially, not just in your investment portfolio or retirement fund, but in every aspect of your financial well-being. You should have good records of all financial and other matters related to you and your family. You should never be disorganized or in disarray about what you have. You are responsible for the management of the money God has entrusted to you. If you don't manage it, it will certainly manage you. Know where you stand financially, being a diligent overseer of the resources God has given you (Prov. 27:23–27).

START INVESTING WITH JUST A LITTLE

God has given to each of us based on how much He knows we can handle. We may not be ones to invest directly in the stock market, but we may invest in other ways. For example, we may invest in mutual funds, exchange-traded funds, or government-investment certificates. Alternatively, we may even choose to stay clear of such investing and take on the world of real estate or become a financial partner in a business.

Whatever level we are, whatever our ability, we can do something with what we have. We may not possess thousands or hundreds of thousands of dollars, but we can start with whatever we have. When God sees our faithfulness in the little we have, He will bless us with more. We should be good stewards and start investing.

Furthermore, we should make God our investment partner. He who supplies the investment seed will also multiply it. So as we invest and see the increase, we should be faithful to sow into the storehouse of God, and He will bless us all the more.

Invest a Little at a Time

If you don't have a lot of funds available to invest, consider the option of dividend reinvestment plans (DRIPs) or purchase mutual funds and exchange-traded funds (ETFs). These investments allow you to purchase small amounts and partial shares or units. With DRIPs, any dividends the company you're invested in pays out are reinvested for you. With mutual funds, you get the benefit of investing in several companies, but the cost is management fees and sometimes sales fees. ETFs mirror stock market or industry performance, but carry a smaller management fee than mutual funds. With any of these you can start small and build bit by bit, and that investment eventually adds up to a lot.

CHAPTER 7

Spend, Spend, Spend: 'Good buy' or 'Good-bye'

We have become consumers rather than customers. Driven by every marketing ploy known and unknown to man, Christians are no different from the unbeliever—going to every sale, buying what they don't need, taking up every new gadget on the market, and sadly teaching their children to want all things instantly. We need to realign our thinking and habits toward spending. We don't need to buy everything we see in the shopping window.

I am not saying this because I am in need, for I have learned to be content whatever the circumstances. I know what it is to be in need, and I know what it is to have plenty. I have learned the secret of being content in any and every situation, whether well fed or hungry, whether living in plenty or in want.

—Philippians 4:11–12 (NIV)

Therefore do not worry, saying, "What shall you eat?" or "What shall we drink?" or "What shall we wear?" For after all these things the Gentiles seek. For your heavenly Father knows that you need all these things. But seek first the kingdom of God and His righteousness, and all these things shall be added to you.

—Matthew 6:31–33

THE "CONSUME ME" AGE

"Consume me. Buy me"—that is the voice that bombards us daily. The society we live in is one of consumption. Television, radio, billboards, store window advertisements, magazines and the like program us to buy. The voices around us call to our attention with "Buy One, Get One Free," "50% Off," "Closing Sale," "Buy Two for $15 Each or One for $20," "Stock Up," "Special Buy," "Save 50%," "Limited Time Offer"—just about anything to get a sale. The ads are so enticing and, for many, hard to resist. Although we want to save and think we'll save by taking advantage of this 'good deal,' we often end up with more than we need or plan for. Sometimes we purchase outside what we can afford using credit cards instead of reducing our high-consumer debt. To convince ourselves it's okay, we give ourselves a little self talk—"It's a good buy"— to justify our spending. For whom is it a good buy—us or the one selling it to us? Most often the greater benefit goes to the seller. The question is, do we really need it? Was it a planned expense? Or is it just that we had to have it? What is it that drives us to consume so much?

Businesses are designed to operate and cater to a world of consumers—and gladly so. Through extensive market research, these organizations develop products and services to transfer the wealth from the consumer to the producer.

Do you realize what the word consume means? To consume is 'to destroy or expend by use; to use up or to spend (money, time, etc.) wastefully; to exhaust; to deplete; to squander or to dissipate'. (For further reference see 'consume', Dictionary.com, s.v. 'consume,' (accessed November 13, 2010), http://dictionary.reference.com/browse/consume.)

Consume means the opposite of produce. It is such a standard word in day-to-day language that we think nothing of it. People are referred to as consumers–those who spend wastefully. Producers of goods and services thrive off this consumer mentality.

We can all agree that we need money to pay for the basic necessities of life. It is also fair to say that apart from these needs, we too can occasionally treat ourselves and others with good gifts. After all, God also wants to give us the desires of our hearts. But some spending reaches beyond these two reasons and is excessive and consuming. Some people buy for reasons that simply do not line up with godly living. Consider the following examples:

* "I like it, so I buy it." Even if buying it means they must charge the purchase and obtain more debt than they can handle.

* "Mary next door got her interlocking tiles for the garage; maybe you should do something similar." The neighbor next door or your friend has one just like it, so you can have one like it too. Of course, it may not even be within your price range, but why not have it anyway? Many have the keeping-up-with-the-Joneses sickness, which often leads to debt (financial death).

* "You don't want to be left out; everybody who's somebody has one or is getting one. Don't get left out!" This may sound like a teenager's words, but it resonates with adults. It's a play on emotions, especially with women. No one wants to feel like he or she doesn't belong.

* "It's the new in thing, the latest and the best." You must have the latest gadget on the market, even if you don't use it.

* "I just gotta have it; I don't care what anybody thinks." Some purchases are the result of outright greed or discontentment—what many already have.

The list of reasons why people overspend could continue, but let's examine a few of them.

Trendy Purchases Still in Your Closets

Maybe you buy the latest designer clothes because you must be in style, not because the clothes in your closet are worn out or no longer fit. You say, "I like it, I buy it." I'm not saying that you should work hard and never reward yourself with something nice, but I am speaking to those who must buy something every week from every sale they can find. Some women and men buy whatever they like, no matter the cost. I know that many are fortunate to have a closet brimming over with clothes; but they haven't worn all of them and probably never will. Have you thought about taking inventory and giving away some of the clothes you haven't worn in years? I'm sure someone will be glad to have that piece you don't like anymore or bought and never wore. One man's trash is another man's treasure. Maybe after you bought that new piece of clothing, you brought it home and decided you don't like it after all. Maybe sometimes you ask yourself why you bought it. What do you do? Nothing. It sits in a bag, goes into a closet, and stays there. If you get a little money conscious, you may return it. However, at times you may find yourself buying another item or two before leaving the store. These are the actions of a consumer.

Please, if you don't need it, return it; or if you're not strapped for cash, then give the clothes to someone in need.

The Latest, the Fastest, the Best

Never has there been a time in history like today when this world has become so technologically advanced and continues to advance. Technological developments have given many benefits and conveniences, yet at the same time they have proven costly to our financial and physical health. People willingly get up in the wee hours of the morning to be the first in line to get the latest electronic gadget that will be obsolete within a few months. They are eager to spend their last dollar or go into debt just to have the latest electronic gadget.

The world has reached the point where no one wants to be disconnected from business, friends, or family. Cell phones, games, computers, and other electronics have more features than those released a few months ago. The producers want you to consume them. What do you do with the old cell phone since you have to get the new release? To make you feel good about your new purchase, the provider may give the option to place it in a recycle program. Isn't that nice? The plan is to get you, the consumer, to buy, and producers will use whatever means necessary to get you on their account. Then, after you've gotten all excited about the bells and whistles of your new phone, you find yourself locked into a one-, two-, or three-year contract that will cost you dearly if you break it. And have you realized that almost every cell phone comes with some kind of data plan? Soon all cell phones will require not only voice but also data. The plan is to get you, the consumer, to spend more. When you look at this computer age, remember this: today it's new, tomorrow it's old.

Computers and the applications we run on them seem to become obsolete the very moment we buy them. Producers have convinced consumers that they should have the best—why settle for less? In our homes, we may have three or more computers, but none of them are fully utilized. Even if we're techies, how can we use all of them efficiently and put them to maximum use? Maybe televisions abound in our homes—one for each room if we can. What is the purpose of having them all?

The Christian Consumer

I have spoken in general terms until now, but let's bring this discussion closer to home. What about those in the body of Christ? Little difference seems to exist between the Christian and the unbeliever as it relates to spending. Some must wear a new outfit every Sunday. Why do we go to church? Is it to serve and worship the Lord, to impress someone, or maybe just to get a little praise from others? Of course, we should make ourselves presentable before God and others—we should dress well—but we don't need a new change of clothes every week. Some feel they can't be seen in the same suit or dress twice. This issue doesn't relate to women alone; some men have more ties than they can count, shirts in every imaginable color, and shoes that look out of this world at some really out-of-this-world prices. We should pause and look into our closets. What haven't we worn lately?

Of course, let's not forget conferences, concerts, and other special events, where we can become convinced that we need every book or CD the speaker presents. Do we really need them? Have we stopped long enough to ask ourselves whether we will use that material anyway? In the midst of the excitement, we may easily buy things we don't need. Have we considered giving those things to someone who can make good use of them? Many buy but do not listen to their CDs, watch their DVDs, or read their books. Sadly, they fail to reap the benefits of the material sitting on their bookshelves.

I love reading and advocate purchasing books or other materials that will help you grow in Christ. Therefore, if you buy it, use it.

Christians have adopted their own form of consumerism. One place I frequent is the Christian bookstore. But I've realized that I'm open to the same temptations of the world, but in a 'religious' way.

How many Bibles do you have on your bookshelf? I'm sure you have more than one. If you are a good student of the Word, you will find that having more than one translation or different types of study Bibles is useful. But some buy Bibles just because they're on sale. Do you have one on your shelf you haven't used? Give it to someone who isn't a Christian.

Christian bookstores have sales for summer, Easter, Christmas—even back-to-school sales for sales' sake. Unfortunately, once the word sale is presented, you have to buy something, even if you don't need it. Maybe you buy books and take them home but sometimes fail to read them. Or maybe you learn nothing from the 'hidden' knowledge sitting on your shelves, waiting to be grasped. So unless you have a purpose for that item in the bookstore, clothing store, or even grocery store, leave it there. You don't need to consume everything.

WHOSE ECONOMY ARE YOU BOOSTING?

Experts estimate the economic forecast of any country based on several factors, including consumer spending. If a demand exists, then producers supply based on the demand. As we often hear, spending drives the economy. But whose economy is prospering? Does excessive spending benefit our economy? What benefit is all this wasteful spending to us? We lose. We spend, we use, and our money is gone. The vicious cycle of consumer spending continues. We earn, we spend, we use, our money is gone, and then we start all over again. This type of excessive spending drives not our economy but the economy of producers. Their profit is our loss.

Let me put it this way; you willingly transfer your wealth to them! Your loss is their gain. Have you ever wondered how an item can be so highly priced, then go on sale for sometimes less than 50 percent of the retail price? Someone is making it big, and it's not you—you operate under the 'it is a good buy' syndrome every time you spend excessively and buy more than necessary. You need to take a lesson from the millionaire next door: "I only buy what I need." It would save you a lot of money and waste.

Rather than boosting the economy of producers and the already wealthy ones who don't know and don't want to serve God, you need to make a paradigm shift. Start thinking about how you can boost your economy and build the kingdom of God through generous giving. Of course, you can start giving generously only if you have a strong economy and more than enough to be a blessing to others.

I believe this is the direction God wants all of us to move toward. So let's see how we can reduce wasteful spending and get right down to having more than enough to be a blessing to others.

HOPE FOR THE BIG SPENDER

Money answers all things. It is the currency by which this world operates. We cannot live on this earth without earning money and spending it on what we need. Both steps are required to function properly in this world. My concern is for those big spenders who go over and above what they need or can afford. To some it may seem fine, but deep inside we know it will lead to disaster. But there is hope for the big spender, and the Word of God may offer more help than we realize.

Too Much, Too Soon

In the familiar story of the prodigal son (Luke 15:11–32), we can see similarities between people living today and people living during Bible times. At the beginning of this story, the younger son of the wealthy man appears as the eager beaver who can't wait to get his hands on his father's money.

Are we eager to have money? Are we always looking for ways to get more and then spend it? Christians often fail in their walk with God because they are focused more on material things or money than on relating to their heavenly Father and becoming more like Christ. Most seek the blessing rather than the One who blesses. No doubt we serve a heavenly Father who is willing to bless us with all things pertaining to life and godliness (2 Peter 1: 3-4). Unfortunately, far too often we cry to Him, "Father, give me this and give me that. Lord, I need a financial blessing," rather than seeking to know Him and making Him known.

In all fairness, this young man asked for what was rightfully his, but his request was premature. Rather than focusing on spending time with his father, his emphasis was on getting his inheritance and deciding what he would do with it. He couldn't wait for his father to die; he wanted his money now. Like this young man, Christians get impatient to wait for the blessing and press God for their financial blessings. In His permissive will, God allows us to receive a blessing, just like this young man's father, knowing fully well that the child is incapable of managing the responsibility financial blessing entails.

Can you identify with this? Have you ever asked God to bless your finances or give you something you thought you really needed, only to realize after receiving it that you were unprepared to handle it? That is what I call 'asking prematurely.' Instead, when you ask for a blessing, you should also ask God to prepare you to handle it when it comes. You should be certain your heart motive is right and that God can trust you with the blessing He gives to you.

One thing is certain—God wants to bless us. However, we do not glorify God if He blesses us and, due to a lack of character, integrity, or money skills, we quickly lose the blessing. For example, why should God promote us to a higher position in an organization, only to be fired shortly afterwards because we couldn't effectively communicate with our colleagues? What glory is there to God if we should come into an inheritance or be given a substantial financial blessing and lose it all within weeks with no way to give account for it?

Have you ever looked back and said to yourself, Oh, I sure wish I had done that differently? Maybe as you look back now, you wish you hadn't spent your money so wildly, especially those large amounts. Maybe you wish you hadn't sold that property so quickly. Maybe you wish you could go back a few years earlier and start afresh. You would love to erase those bad financial decisions you made along the way. Whatever it is, you realize it was too much too soon, and you failed to consult God about what to do. However, there is hope.

Spend It All

Within days of receiving his inheritance, this young man packed up and left home. He no longer had anyone to guide him. He went as far as he could from his father. His only companion was his possessions. Along the way he met people who gladly helped him spend his inheritance. As the saying goes, "Easy come, easy go." He wasted away all that his father had labored hard to provide for him. He wasted his inheritance. He wasted his blessing.

We may not be coming into an inheritance, but God has given blessings, and we have often wasted them. We daily use our work, education, strength, ingenuity, and all that we are in exchange for money, but then we have wasted it on frivolous spending. We may have enjoyed many good things in our lives on account of our efforts; however, all we have comes from God. All we have is a blessing from our heavenly Father.

Yet when we receive our paycheck or money for services rendered, instead of asking God what to do with it and making a plan for it, our first act is to spend. Instead of setting aside our tithe, offerings, and savings, we first spend on whatever we want. We spend as we please because, the way we see it, we worked hard for it and deserve it. After we have spent to our heart's content, reality sets in. As is the usual routine, we realize too late that we lack enough money to pay the bills and cover our living expenses. This is the vicious cycle of the big spender that ends sadly.

As in the case of this young man, the money strangely evaporates from our bank account—more quickly than it took for us to earn it. If we're truthful with ourselves, we'll recognize that our paycheck is spent in only a few hours to a few days. Sad to say, we have no respect for what it took to earn that money—even though we're the ones who worked for it.

Have we ever considered how much our parents have invested in us, how many hours we have studied and worked, or the number of times we've prayed and others have prayed for us to be blessed? If we did even a simple calculation of how long it takes to earn one dollar, we'd be more appreciative of and careful about how we spend our money.

Come to Your Senses

What do you spend your money on? Do you spend your money on more clothes, shoes, electronic gadgets, dinners out with friends, another family event, or anything you see on sale? Are you spending your money on what doesn't satisfy (Isa. 55:2)? Are you happy when you have spent all or sometimes more than what you have earned? You should take care that after all the extravagant living you don't end up like this young man.

After he wasted his inheritance, hard times came,

and the economy fell. Sound familiar, doesn't it? Maybe you can identify with this guy. Excessive spending and high consumer debt, along with world financial market turmoil, have left many in want. Without houses, cars, jobs, and savings, many face great uncertainty about the future. His prodigal living resulted in his being worse off than the servants in his father's house. While those servants had a roof over their heads, a bed to sleep in, and good food to eat, he lived with pigs and ate pig food! How low can you get? Perhaps you've hit rock bottom and will do anything to survive or make ends meet. For some, that means getting into more debt or another credit card, but that just adds to their problem.

Take a page from this young man's story and consider how it applies to you. You need to recognize what you have done and be willing to change direction. Being a big spender may have put you in a difficult financial position with too many bills to pay, creditors calling you constantly, and insufficient money to cover your daily living expenses. But hope remains.

This young man recognized that being in his father's house as a servant was far better than living in his current position. At least he would have shelter and food. He was willing to return, as shameful as it would have felt, to seek his father's forgiveness. He was willing to go to his father, admit his faults, and ask to be restored.

What about you? Do you realize that being in the Father's house and eating His bread as His servant are much better than eating pig food? In other words, do you realize that when you live in God's house and serve Him, eat His word, and align your life to His will, you will no longer struggle through life? You will find that His Word prepares you for every aspect of life, lifts you up, and restores you, including your finances. In His house His Word satisfies; there you will find help to eliminate the habit of overspending. You need to realign your life, including the habit of excessive spending, to His will. Are you ready to acknowledge your sin and return to the Father? If you confess to the Father that you are a spendthrift and ask for His forgiveness, He will certainly forgive you and also help you to live victoriously above that sin of overspending (1 John 1:9).

Right now, pause and take a moment to go to the Father and ask for His forgiveness (Luke 15:18), just like this young man did. The Father is waiting with open arms for you to return and surrender this area of your life to Him. He will receive you, celebrate with you, and give you the ability to overcome the habit of overspending. Give it all to Jesus; He is able to help you.

Be assured that the Father has forgiven you. The beauty of this story is found in the father's response to the return of his lost son. He celebrated his return. His return signified the son's acknowledgment of his faults, his helplessness, and the need for his father's forgiveness. His father's response with open arms, the celebration with the killing of the fatted calf, and the giving of the signet ring, robe and sandals, signifies restoration. He wanted his son to know that he was forgiven and accepted as his son once again. This forgiveness symbolizes the love God has for you and me. Whenever you fall, you can come back to the Father. God will completely restore your life, including your finances.

PRACTICAL HELPS TO ELIMINATE EXCESSIVE SPENDING

Being practical is good. We need to do our part to ensure that we do not fall into the temptation of overspending, which has too many repercussions—not just financially but also emotionally. Financially, we may find ourselves strapped down with more debt and a long time period to get out of it. Emotionally, we become disappointed or feel guilty when we slip and fall into the temptation of overspending. Therefore, for our own benefit, we ought to put some guards in place to help us win this battle.

Make a List Before You Go Shopping

Sometimes I can get carried away in the grocery store, so before I leave home I determine what I need and how much I'm willing or can afford to spend. This list keeps me from buying unnecessary items that often stay in the freezer and are unused. I also plan my week of meals and buy only what I need for that period. Most importantly, I keep God in my daily activities, including my spending. I set my plans before Him and ask Him to direct me in everything I do.

Question Yourself

Perhaps you see items on sale in the grocery store. Before you pick up more than one of the same item, ask yourself, Am I going to use all of these before they spoil? Is this a good item to stock up on? Will this item likely be on sale in the near future? Sometimes you may purchase sale items that will expire soon and would be useless before you get to use them. Watch out for this problem, especially when food items are at very low prices. Also beware of items that can be easily frozen; perhaps your freezer is so loaded with food that you are unaware of what is in them! If you are observant of sale patterns, you'll notice that some items tend to go on sale at certain times during the year and often more than once. If you can refrain from making the extra purchase, do so to keep your cash flow free. Often you may not realize that though storing up on certain items may be good, it also means reducing cash flow that could be otherwise used for some other need. Questioning yourself will help reduce unnecessary purchases.

Take Stock

Before your next visit to the clothing store, take inventory of your closet and decide what you will keep, give away, or toss. You may be convinced you don't have anything to wear to a certain special event, but maybe you can use something sitting in your closet. Maybe you just need a blouse, shirt, pants, or accessories to go with something you already have. The temptation to buy something new can cause you to spend money you should otherwise keep. Perhaps you end up making impulsive purchases or buy what you probably won't wear again. In addition to clothing, women often think they need a new hairstyle for a special occasion. Before you realize how much you've spent, the occasion comes and goes, but the debt remains. Watch those special occasions or celebrations; buying something new isn't always a need. One little addition or change can make the old or slightly worn seem completely new to the eyes you want to impress.

Another caution is to be wary of outlet stores. Not all have reduced prices, and some entice you to buy more than one of the same type of clothing when one would suffice. For the store the goal is to get rid of the old stock before bringing in newer items. If each person buys two of the same item instead of one, the store profits more quickly. Do you really want two or more of the same item in your closet? Don't let these stores entice you to buy more than you need.

You Don't Need to Buy Everything You See in the Shopping Window

Remind yourself of this truth and teach your children at an early age that they cannot have it all. When your children go shopping with you, sometimes deny them or put a limit on what they are allowed to have. Help them make good decisions about purchases. For example, while grocery shopping, some children have a tendency to pick up what they like and put it in the cart. Give children the option to choose one of those items and ask them why they made that choice. This practice will help them make better decisions about their purchases. If they fuss at all, they should not be entitled to anything. Refuse to be a weak parent and decide not to go back on this guideline later. Leave the item in the store.

I started this practice with my child at the early age of two and a half. The store attendants were either annoyed or amused, perhaps thinking I was being a difficult parent or that practicing good financial skills with mom and daughter was 'cute.'

I have noticed that those early years of saying no or making her choose have helped her make better choices. Sometimes to my surprise, my daughter refuses an item with the comment, "I don't think I need that now. You can wait until later." Other times I see that though she would like me to buy her something, she refrains from asking. Children are not too young to learn and practice good management skills.

Receive and Give at the Same Time

Each time you and your children receive a new gift, make a practice of giving up two or more of a similar item. As your children lose interest in their toys, give those toys away.

If you took a serious look at how much waste is in our children's rooms alone—if you put a dollar value on those items—you may shudder. Refuse to turn your child into a consumer; train him or her early to be a responsible money manager.

Our lives are about giving, not just getting and having. Hoarding habits develop easily—we buy something, keep or put it aside for another time, but never use it. Then we buy storage containers to keep the items we never use. We are accumulating, not using. This consumer-driven society has developed hoarders. People have more than they need and not enough space to store it. This problem, of course, benefits those who provide storage facilities so we can keep stuff we don't need and will never use. We need to avoid hoarding and wasteful spending.

Save toward Your Next Big Purchase

No matter how small it is, save from every source of income, not just your paycheck. A little becomes a lot over time. Eliminating excessive spending requires a change of habit. Replace the habit of spending with the habit of saving. Saving is a habit that requires both discipline and diligence. It also forces you to deny fulfilling your wants right away. When you develop the habit of saving, you begin to bring stability to your financial life.

Save with a goal in mind. Certainly save for the golden years, but also save for short-terms goals such as vacations, important family events, or the big-ticket item you would like or will soon need to replace. When you purchase with cash rather than credit, you reap the greater reward of peace. The habit of saving goes a long way toward helping you eliminate the habit of excessive spending.

Get an accountability partner. Find a Christian friend who is good at managing money, someone you can trust to help you on this journey. You may also consider joining a group that focuses on reducing debt and eliminating bad spending habits or managing money as a whole. In all this, seek God's guidance on whom you can trust to help you through this financial challenge. If you socialize with friends for whom spending money is the norm, reduce or eliminate them from your social calendar. You're in a better position when you befriend those with whom you can pray or study the Word of God. Apart from having good company, occupy yourself with an alternative activity rather than going to the mall 'just because.' Consider joining a ministry or volunteering in a charitable organization that would occupy most of your free (shopping) time. When you have limited time available for shopping, you become very focused on what you need—you go in the store, pick what you need, and leave without spending extra. Furthermore, being in the house of God or a good service is better than wasting away your hard-earned money. If you have no specific reason for being in a shopping mall, stay away. If you need to go, make plans to take your accountability partner, who can help keep you in line.

The Spender's Prayer

This may sound strange, but pray that God will take away your desire to spend beyond your needs (especially if you are in a financial crunch). It works. In addition, ask Him to do this in the heart of your spouse and children as well. This will help relieve pressure from you and those around you the most. Also think back to when you spent more than necessary. How did you feel? Was something troubling you? Did you spend more when you were with friends or certain family members? Did you feel pressured to spend? Identifying when you spend excessively will also help you determine when not to go shopping, thus reducing or eliminating this problem. In all you do, ask God to help you overcome this habit.

CHAPTER 8

Give:
A Different Type of Investment

Sadly, the majority of North American Christians, especially those in the higher income bracket, do not give. Approximately 20 percent of those in any congregation are faithful at tithing and giving. We need to realign our money management to include more giving that has eternal value.

Give, and it will be given to you: good measure, pressed down, shaken together, and running over will be put into your bosom. For with the same measure that you use, it will be measured back to you.

—Luke 6:38

Everything comes from you; all we're doing is giving back what we've been given from your generous hand.

—1 Chronicles 29:14b (MSG)

WHY CHRISTIANS BUT NOT GIVERS?

Reconciling the two—being Christians but not givers—is hard, yet this is the reality for many who profess Christianity as their way of life. Research shows that less than 50 percent of church members faithfully tithe or give. Of that 50 percent, the majority are in the low income bracket, making an annual income of less than twenty thousand dollars. Looking closely at these statistics, we see that a high percentage of those who give earn less than those who don't give or give very little. We can review websites on Canadian and American giving statistics compiled by the Charities File on Board and by Generous Giving (http://thecharitiesfile.ca/en/fastfacts and http://www.generousgiving.org/stats#respectively).

Not giving is a big problem for many Christians, who have the world of excuses about why they can't or shouldn't give to God. Their reasons for not giving are based on the condition of their hearts rather than on the size of their bank accounts.

Why don't we give? Or why do we give so little? What are our reasons or excuses for lack of giving? Here are a few possible options.

1. You Hold Back What You Should Give

There is one who scatters, yet increases more; and there is one who withholds more than is right, but it leads to poverty.

—Proverbs 11:24

The Word of God says some people withhold more than is necessary. They don't mind giving, but it must be totally on their terms. Such are unwilling to heed the Spirit of God's promptings to give more. This withholding spirit has become prevalent among believers, and as such, many have failed to experience the blessings of God in their lives. What is the withholding spirit? When we have committed to give a certain amount but do not—this grieves the Holy Spirit. The story of Ananias and Sapphira (Acts 4:32–37; 5:1–11) gives a clear example of withholding more than is necessary.

When you function in the grip of this withholding spirit, money has a stronghold in your life. Money becomes your god. It doesn't matter whether you are rich or poor; money can control you. You either don't think you have enough to give or love money so much that you can't let it go. When you have control over money or anything else in life, you find it easy to let it go. When someone else controls you, however, doing right proves difficult, even though you know you need to do the right thing.

The attitude some believe is justifiable is this: "It's my money. I earned it." It's your money only because God allowed you to have it and gave it to you to manage wisely. Part of managing what He has given to you includes giving judiciously. Please don't allow money to control you. Control it, be its boss, and send it where God instructs you to.

2. You Fear You Won't Have Enough

Some fear that if they give from their small amount, they won't have enough left to meet their needs. This conclusion is certainly untrue. I can testify from my personal life that when you give, even when times are tough, God takes care of your needs.

At one time I could give without feeling the pinch. Then a family problem resulted in a major depletion of our financial resources. This trial tested my faith in God, and I had to put all my trust in Him and His promise to keep me. I decided that no matter how challenging life became, I would continue to tithe and give offerings. I took it upon myself to adhere to Scripture and fully believed I should never go into the presence of God empty-handed (Ex. 23:15; Deut. 16:16). The financial challenge I faced meant that bills were paid late. Sometimes I didn't know whether the mortgage would be paid on time, and I often went without any cash in my purse. I recall times when my refrigerator and cupboards had hardly anything in them. I went to church or home group meetings and gave an offering, no matter how much or little I had (even if that meant giving all the change left in my wallet).

Through it all, God has been faithful to His Word. I can recall the many times God intervened on my behalf. I often received a gift of money just in time to pay the mortgage payment that was coming due. My tax refund came before the estimated time to receive it. I have never been without enough food to feed my family. Even when I didn't have something to cook, someone always invited me for dinner or gave me groceries. I know that during all those times God was intervening on my behalf and taking care of me. I'm even certain of it because I didn't make my financial situation known to others, yet God touched the heart of others to bless me when I was in need. Certainly I can say like David in Psalm 37:25, "I have been young, and now am old; yet I have not seen the righteous forsaken, nor his descendants begging bread."

You may think you won't be able to survive if you give to the Lord, but you will. You may be giving and saying to yourself that you're not seeing the blessings of the Lord on your life, but daily He blesses you. Furthermore, you will find that if you give willingly and cheerfully from a pure, sincere, and thankful heart, the Lord will remember you and keep you in the day of trouble and protect you just because you have faithfully given to Him. Your giving will cause God to copiously provide all your needs from His unlimited riches. Give, even when the going gets tough. God will take care of you.

3. You Fail to See Giving as a Blessing

I have shown you in every way, by laboring like this, that you must support the weak. And remember the words of the Lord Jesus, that He said, "It is more blessed to give than to receive."

—Acts 20:35

Believers often fail to see the blessedness of giving. They often fail to take God at His Word and believe that just as the person who receives the gift is blessed, the one who gives it is blessed even more.

Luke 6:38 commands us to give and promises that we will receive much more in return, but for many, this is just a popular saying. But we act like unbelievers because that Word goes in one ear and out the other without penetrating our hearts. We fail to believe and hence are blind to any blessing in giving because we don't expect any. We do not even know the joy or pleasure of giving to someone in need as a blessing. We don't trust God enough to give back to Him, whether in the form of a tithe, regular weekly offering, or other form of charitable giving. Yet no farmer plants a seed without expecting a harvest. No one invests in business or the markets without expecting a return. Therefore, no Christian should plant a gift without expecting a gift in return. If God says He will bless the giver more than the receiver, if He says the giver will receive much more than he or she gave, then we should give with expectation. We should give and expect a harvest.

4. You Don't Tithe, so You Don't Give

Will a man rob God? Yet you have robbed Me! But you say, "In what way have we robbed You?" In tithes and offerings.

—Malachi 3:8

Many in the body of Christ despise this Scripture. In Malachi, Israel was giving to the Lord; however, their tithing and giving were flawed. Although they gave even with tears, their giving was partial and ceremonial. It was not out of love for God. In other words, they did the right thing but with the wrong motives. They gave in part, but not the whole. To God partial obedience is complete disobedience.

Many can't give because they have no love for God or His people. Many tithe, but in part. This lack of tithing or partial tithing results in a lack of freewill giving or offerings.

If you lack the discipline to tithe, then giving would prove difficult to do. Those who don't tithe find giving even a little difficult. If you haven't developed the habit of tithing and saving, then developing the habit of giving will be a challenge. Whenever you tithe, bring the whole tithe. Whenever you give, give willingly as you purpose in your heart to give. Never hold back.

5. You Are Too Financially Stretched to Give

"God will understand if I don't give." How many times have you made that excuse or heard someone say it? As the saying goes, "You have a bandage for every sore." You always have a valid reason for not giving. Perhaps you have too many responsibilities to consider giving, or maybe you lack sufficient payment for your work to be able to give. Yet those who give also lack, and they have neither died from lacking funds nor been left out on the street. God takes care of them. Furthermore, those who love giving always seem to have more than enough to give. God funnels money to them so they can be blessings to others.

Maybe you are a big spender. If you spend more than you earn before you take out your tithe and savings or before you consider all your necessary living expenses, you will not have enough to give toward any good or charitable cause. Too much irresponsible spending and debt holds you in a prison that prohibits you from living and giving freely. Many often cry, "I'm up to my ears in debt. I can't give now." It's time for you to get out of debt and get into giving and living for God.

6. You Desire to Give But Lack the Resources

I have noticed that some truly love the Lord Jesus and strongly desire to give but lack the resources. That being the case, maybe you should examine your financial condition and position to see if you can adjust any areas to make finances available for the work of the Lord. You may see the necessity of making additional income if you desire to be financially free so you can give. At the same time this step would rid you of any debt burden that has been the prevailing cause of limited finances. If your heart's desire is to give, you need to put that desire into action and work on ways to give. As the saying goes, "Where there's a will, there's a way." With God's help you will be able to give as you desire.

7. You Harbor Wrong Thinking about Who Receives Your Gift

No matter how long the church has been in existence, the misconception that we give to man rather than to God still runs rampant in the body of Christ. Even though we write our checks to a specific organization, put our offerings in the church offering bowl, or give to a friend or some other charitable organization, we give our gifts to the Lord.

God commands us in Malachi 3:10, "Bring ye all the tithes into the storehouse, that there may be meat in mine house, and prove me now herewith, saith the Lord of hosts, if I will not open you the windows of heaven, and pour you out a blessing, that there shall not be room enough to receive it" (KJV). In other words, bring your gifts to church so those in need will be blessed. The meat in the storehouse is for the pastor so he would have enough for his household needs and be equipped to bless the congregation with the Word (spiritual meat) from

God (Num. 18:21). The meat in the storehouse is also for the people of the congregation (Deut. 14:27–29). It helps to feed those who lack enough, sends missionaries to remote places to preach the gospel, builds hospitals and schools where needed, and does work that supports the vision of the Lord has given to the pastor.

In short, the people of the Lord give the meat of the storehouse to the Lord for the sake of the people. The book of Acts is filled with examples of the early church's practice of giving that supports Malachi 3:10. These early Christians gave and distributed among themselves so no one would lack anything but have his or her needs supplied. Today, the body of Christ should be doing the same thing.

In Matthew 25:34–40, Jesus explained that Christians will be judged based on their character as revealed by their charitable deeds. Jesus told us that our charitable deeds or giving to others is, in fact, toward Him.

> *Then shall the King say unto them on his right hand, Come, ye blessed of my Father, inherit the kingdom prepared for you from the foundation of the world: for I was an hungred, and ye gave me meat: I was thirsty, and ye gave me drink: I was a stranger, and ye took me in: naked, and ye clothed me: I was sick, and ye visited me: I was in prison, and ye came unto me. Then shall the righteous answer him, saying, Lord, when saw we thee an hungred, and fed thee? or thirsty, and gave thee drink? When saw we thee a stranger, and took thee in? or naked, and clothed thee? Or when saw we thee sick, or in prison,*

and came unto thee? And the King shall answer and say unto them, Verily I say unto you, Inasmuch as ye have done it unto one of the least of these my brethren, ye have done it unto me.

—Matthew 25:34–40 (KJV)

We are judged not so much for the act of giving, but for the inner condition of our hearts. As Christians, if we stand on the name of Christ, our outward acts of giving should reflect our inward character of righteousness. Rest assured, our giving will be rewarded. When we give to others, we must remember that we are ultimately giving the gift to Him. When we give, we should give as unto the Lord—our gift is not to a person, organization, or church. The ultimate receiver of our gift is God.

WHAT CAN YOUR GIFT DO?

In the song "And the Gift Goes On," Ron Harris and Claire Cloninger tell the story of how one gift can keep on giving from generation to generation. The gift of love that began with God the Father still continues today in our hearts by the Spirit of God, who lives in us. Giving has a ripple effect. We may think we're giving to an individual or charity, and that's the end of it—but our gift goes on. When we give, we should know that our gift of love will bless more people than we may ever know.

We cannot fully understand how much we bless others when we give to help them. When we give, we invest in the lives of others—an investment that has eternal value. On account of our giving, a life is preserved from death. We give hope to someone, cause someone to give God thanks, and reignite someone's trust in God. We can help educate someone, feed someone, fund research for an incurable sickness, build a hospital, send water to a village in desperate need, send preachers to remote areas to spread the gospel, and bring healing to the sick. Our giving can do so much to help others. This is why we should give.

Giving is not only a benefit to those who receive it but a different type of investment that brings a return to the giver that far outweighs the gift. From the world's perspective, investing brings the expectation of receiving some anticipated return for the amount we've invested—whether time, money, or skill. For any investment, the risk associated with it helps an investor decide whether he or she will make an investment. From the Christian worldview, giving as an investment has far more benefits than the risks involved. Jesus promises that when we give, we will receive in return far more than we gave (Luke 6:38). Giving is reciprocal—it comes back to us. Giving creates a void God will by all means fill for us. God will look into our lives to see what we need or desire and ensure it is given to us. He also promises in Acts 20:35 that the giver will be blessed more than the receiver. When we take God's view of giving, it is hard to determine whether any risk is involved in the investment of giving to Him and others. Scripture is filled with examples of men and women who were givers. When we examine their lives, we see that clearly their giving never matched God's. For sure, giving provokes God to do the extraordinary in our lives.

Giving Blesses Beyond Your Generation

Now it came to pass when the king was dwelling in his house, and the Lord had given him rest from all his enemies all around, that the king said to Nathan the prophet, "See now, I dwell in a house of cedar, but the ark of God dwells inside tent curtains." Then Nathan said to the king, "Go, do all that is in your heart, for the Lord is with you." But it happened that night that the word of the Lord came to Nathan, saying, "Go and tell My servant David, 'Thus says the Lord: "Would you build a house for Me to dwell in? For I have not dwelt in a house since the time that I brought the children of Israel up from Egypt, even to this day, but have moved about in a tent and in a tabernacle. Wherever I have moved about with all the children of Israel, have I ever spoken a word to anyone from the tribes of Israel, whom I commanded to shepherd My people Israel, saying, 'Why have you not built Me a house of cedar?'" Now therefore, thus shall you say to My servant David, 'Thus says the Lord of hosts: "I took you from the sheepfold, from following the sheep, to be ruler over My people, over Israel. And I have been with you wherever you have gone, and have cut off all your enemies from before you, and have made you a great name, like the name of the great men who are on the earth. Moreover I will appoint a place for My people Israel, and will plant them, that they may dwell in a place of their own and move no more; nor shall the sons of wickedness oppress them anymore, as previously, since the time that I commanded judges to be over My people Israel, and have caused you to rest from all your enemies. Also the Lord tells you that He will make you a house. When your days are fulfilled and you rest with your fathers, I will set up your seed after you, who will come from your body, and I will establish his kingdom. He shall build a house for My name, and I will establish the throne of his kingdom forever. I will be his Father, and he shall be My son. If he commits iniquity, I will chasten him with the rod of men and with the blows of the sons of men. But My mercy shall not depart from him, as I took it from Saul, whom I removed from before you. And your house and your kingdom shall be established forever before you. Your throne shall be established forever."' According to all these words and according to all this vision, so Nathan spoke to David.

—2 Samuel 7:1–17

David desired to honor God for all He had done for him. God had promoted him from a shepherd boy to a king, seen him through many hardships, and given him peace from his enemies. David wanted to honor God by building a house for the ark of the covenant. This desire touched God so much that He established David's throne forever. Even when David fell into sin and his sons fought against him, God kept His covenant with David through Christ.

David had not yet performed the act of giving, yet God was willing to bless him because he wanted to give. Have you ever thought of giving a special gift to God, then received more than what you expected and was able to give as you desired? When your heart's desire is for God and giving to His work, He will bring opportunities to bless you so you can give as you desire. Sometimes we frown when pastors ask for gifts for a new church building or for other worthy projects; however, we should view such opportunities as a means of honoring God. We should be happy to participate in these projects because our giving is to the Lord and not to man.

Although God told David that he wouldn't allow him to build the house because he was a man of war, this didn't deter him from participating in the process. David gladly prepared his offering for the house that would one day be built in God's honor.

This act teaches a valuable lesson. When you make a commitment to give or do something for God, do it (read 1 Chron. 29). Not only was David's offering for the house of God great, it also caused the people who assembled before him to give willingly. David's giving has brought blessings for many generations because King Jesus reigns upon this throne. God's gift to David far outweighed what David gave—to have his throne established forever. What a gift for giving to God!

Giving Brings Wisdom and Riches

> *And Solomon loved the Lord, walking in the statutes of his father David, except that he sacrificed and burned incense at the high places. Now the king went to Gibeon to sacrifice there, for that was the great high place: Solomon offered a thousand burnt offerings on that altar. At*

Gibeon the Lord appeared to Solomon in a dream by night; and God said, "Ask! What shall I give you?" And Solomon said: "You have shown great mercy to Your servant David my father, because he walked before You in truth, in righteousness, and in uprightness of heart with You; You have continued this great kindness for him, and You have given him a son to sit on his throne, as it is this day. Now, O Lord my God, You have made Your servant king instead of my father David, but I am a little child; I do not know how to go out or come in. And Your servant is in the midst of Your people whom You have chosen, a great people, too numerous to be numbered or counted. Therefore give to Your servant an understanding heart to judge Your people, that I may discern between good and evil. For who is able to judge this great people of Yours?"

The speech pleased the Lord, that Solomon had asked this thing. Then God said to him: "Because you have asked this thing, and have not asked long life for yourself, nor have asked riches for yourself, nor have asked the life of your enemies, but have asked for yourself understanding to discern justice, behold, I have done according to your words; see, I have given you a wise and understanding heart, so that there has not been anyone like you before you, nor shall any like you arise after you. And I have also given you what you have not asked: both riches and honor, so that there shall not be anyone like you among the kings all your days. So if you walk in My ways, to keep My statutes and My commandments, as your father David walked, then I will lengthen your days." Then Solomon awoke; and indeed it had been a dream. And he came to Jerusalem and stood before the ark of the covenant of the Lord, offered up burnt offerings, offered peace offerings, and made a feast for all his servants.

—1 Kings 3:3–15

Solomon was a young king with a heart for God. Solomon loved God and displayed this love through the offering of sacrifices. He offered to God far more than what was required of him. His giving so touched God's heart that God presented him with a blank check: "Ask! What shall I give you?"

What if God visited you like this? Would you know what to ask for, or would you be dumbfounded or lost for words? Solomon had an answer to this open-ended question, and his request was not a small one either—to be wise, to be able to discern good and evil, and to judge people fairly. His prayer pleased God so much that God gave him not only what he asked for but more. God gave Solomon the gift of wisdom that exceeded the wisdom of any other person (then and now). He also received not only riches but also honor far above the kings of his day—and with obedience, God promised a long life. Both Solomon's outlandish giving and prayers pleased God.

Does your giving please God enough for Him to answer your prayers in a way that's exceedingly above what you ask? Do your prayer requests please God? Solomon's prayer wasn't about himself but about pleasing God. It wasn't about himself only but about helping others. Yes, he wanted wisdom, but not for himself alone that he should live a better life. He desired wisdom for the people God had ordained him to lead.

Are your prayers only about you or about others? If you model Solomon's example to give more than necessary at times and ask with others in mind (and not just for yourself), you would do well to receive from God far more than you ask.

Giving Brings Life Again

At Joppa there was a certain disciple named Tabitha, which is translated Dorcas. This woman was full of good works and charitable deeds which she did. But it happened in those days that she became sick and died. When they had washed her, they laid her in an upper room. And since Lydda was near Joppa, and the disciples had heard that Peter was there, they sent two men to him, imploring him not to delay in coming to them. Then Peter arose and went with them. When he had come, they brought him to the upper room. And all the widows stood by him weeping, showing the tunics and garments which Dorcas had made while she was with them. But Peter put them all out, and knelt down and prayed. And turning to the body he said, "Tabitha, arise." And she opened her eyes, and when she saw Peter she sat up. Then he gave her his hand and lifted her up; and when he had called the saints and widows, he presented her alive. And it became known throughout all Joppa, and many believed on the Lord.

—Acts 9:36–42

Dorcas was a loving giver. The Bible describes her as a woman full of good works and charitable deeds. She was one who gave to help improve the lives of others, particularly widows. This should be the joy of any Christian person. Her sudden death was met with great sorrow, and an urgent plea was sent to Peter to pray for her. The outcry of the community came because of who Dorcas was—a giver, someone who touched many lives through her generosity.

Have you ever asked yourself these questions? When I have passed from this earth, or if I should move from my community to another, will I be missed? Will people mourn my passing? Am I impacting lives positively where I live now? Do people see me as generous or stingy?

It is certain that had it not been for Dorcas's giving, Peter would not have been called to the scene. Peter's prayer restored Dorcas's life and caused a community to rejoice again and for others to come into the kingdom of God. Psalm 41:3 assures us that God remembers the one who gives when he or she falls sick. One of the 'returns' of giving is healing or restored health and strength.

You may not fall sick like Dorcas, but maybe you have situations in your life where restoration is needed. Your restored life may serve as an instrument to lead others to Christ. Dorcas's restored life not only benefited her, but also caused many to believe in the Lord. Her life was one that kept on giving.

Giving Brings Salvation

There was a certain man in Caesarea called Cornelius, a

centurion of what was called the Italian Regiment, a devout man and one who feared God with all his household, who gave alms generously to the people, and prayed to God always. About the ninth hour of the day he saw clearly in a vision an angel of God coming in and saying to him, "Cornelius!" And when he observed him, he was afraid, and said, "What is it, lord?" So he said to him, "Your prayers and your alms have come up for a memorial before God. Now send men to Joppa, and send for Simon whose surname is Peter. He is lodging with Simon, a tanner, whose house is by the sea. He will tell you what you must do." And when the angel who spoke to him had departed, Cornelius called two of his household servants and a devout soldier from among those who waited on him continually. So when he had explained all these things to them, he sent them to Joppa.

—Acts 10:1–8

Much is said of this man Cornelius—an Italian soldier, a religious man who feared the Lord, and a generous giver. Cornelius was just like Dorcas; he put his faith in action by giving to the poor. Cornelius's prayers, plus his giving, got God's attention (Acts 10:4, 31). God not only visited him in a vision but, also opened the door for the gospel to be preached to him and his family. He and his family received the gospel, and also the outpouring of the Holy Spirit was upon them.

When you add giving to your prayers, God is bound to pay attention and do something new and wonderful in your life and in the lives of your family. Giving can bring salvation.

Giving Refreshes You

There is a story which I have heard many times that reminds me that no matter what, God keeps those who are His. It goes like this.

During her early years in Canada, a woman worked for a family as a live-in nanny. Unfortunately for her, the mistress of the house was sometimes mean and unreasonable. One day she asked the live-in nanny to take her children out for breakfast and told her to make sure to eat breakfast with them. When they returned home, the mistress of the household told her (for whatever reason) that she would not have dinner with them in the evening. Rather, she should prepare it, clean up after them, and then go to her room. By evening she was obviously hungry, but couldn't go out to eat because she had limited funds. She sat in her room praying that God would send help. Faithfully, God did.

Soon there was someone knocking at her door. A woman whom she didn't know very well brought food for her, and it was her favorite dish. As she received this gift of food with tears and thanksgiving, she remembered her grandmother. You see, her grandmother had a tendency to give to others and often gave more than seemed necessary, leaving the family with little. This nanny would often complain, but her grandmother reiterated that one day she would pass away, but her giving would bring help to her one day. The woman who brought the bowl of food was one to whom her grandmother had always given. At the prompting of the Lord, she showed up with that meal. Certainly the Lord refreshed this nanny with a much-needed meal. As Proverbs 11:24–25 says, "There is one who scatters, yet increases more; and there is one who withholds more than is right, but it leads to poverty. The generous soul will be made rich, and he who waters will also be watered himself."

Often you may not see the benefits of your giving right away, but those blessings will come back to you, your children, or other members of your family.

In the examples above, the blessings God gave to each of these people extended beyond themselves, their families, their friends, and their generation. Who knows what your giving will do now and in the future? Give and it shall be given in ways too great for you to imagine. Giving blesses beyond your life.

THE HOW-TO OF GIVING

You have seen how giving can be a blessing to yourself and others. It is clear that you cannot out-give God, yet He expects you to give. As you read through Scripture, you will also recognize ways in which you should give. Giving revolves around the condition of your heart.

Although most know how to give, reviewing some of these guidelines can only help to reinforce our understanding of the giving process.

Give Out of Obedience to God

Giving is a command. When we look through Scripture, we see that God doesn't say we should not give. He clearly expects us to give. Giving is quite similar to praying. The point is not if you pray but when you pray. Praying daily is a normal part of the Christian walk. The point is not if you give but when you give. Giving should be part of every Christian's lifestyle and done out of obedience to the Lord Jesus. Jesus said in Luke 6:30, "Give to everyone who asks you, and if anyone takes what belongs to you, do not demand it back" (NIV). Also in Luke 6:38, He said, "Give, and it will be given to you. A good measure, pressed down, shaken together and running over, will be poured into your lap. For with the measure you use, it will be measured to you" (NIV). If you need a starting point to determine whether you should give, let that be obedience to God.

Give Out of Love for God and His People

If you're not giving, what's the meaning of your life? If God Himself gives and you are made in His image and likeness, then you should also be a giver. God gives out of love for His own, and as His child you should also give to Him and others out of love. The saying often repeated among believers is true: "You can give without loving, but you can never love without giving." Giving is the currency of love. It is a by-product of your love for God and others.

Give Generously, Even with a Little

The measure of your generosity is based not on how much you give compared to someone else, but according to what is left after you've given from what you have. The woman who gave the mites gave all she had. Though it was small compared to what others gave, the Lord considered her gift more valuable than that of the others. Why? She gave all she had—"her whole livelihood."

> Now Jesus sat opposite the treasury and saw how the people put money into the treasury. And many who were rich put in much. Then one poor widow came and threw in two mites, which make a quadrans. So He called His disciples to Himself and said to them, "Assuredly, I say to you that this poor widow has put in more than all those who have given to the treasury; for they all put in out of their abundance, but she out of her poverty put in all that she had, her whole livelihood."

—Mark 12:41–44

Some give out of abundance, but cannot give when faced with financial difficulties. The act of giving during a time of lack shows the condition of the heart—we love God and trust Him for our needs. We should make every effort to give, no matter what the state of our finances may be.

Give Willingly and Cheerfully

So often we hear that we should give willingly and

cheerfully, but for some that means nothing. We should rejoice in the Lord that we have the ability to give— whether toward the work of the Lord or to bless someone. Giving is a privilege some do not have. In 1 Chronicles 29, David prayed a beautiful prayer that expresses the heart of every giver—we are giving to God willingly. We should give willingly and with rejoicing, knowing that we are giving back part of our substance to the great God of heaven and earth, who has blessed us. Also Paul encourages the church in 2 Corinthians 9:7, "So let each one give as he purposes in his heart, not grudgingly or of necessity; for God loves a cheerful giver." We should let our giving attitude please God.

Plan Your Giving

God wants you neither to go through life empty-handed (Ex. 3:21) nor to come into His presence empty-handed (Deut. 16:15-17). You should go neither into the house of the Lord nor to any place where the body of Christ is gathered without an offering.

This being the case, you should make a practice of planning your giving. As soon as you receive money— whether from your job, other income source, or gift—set aside the tithe to pay to the Lord. Apart from that, determine on a weekly basis what you will give before you enter into the house of God for worship. Paul encouraged the church to do this in 1 Corinthians 16:2. Since giving is free will, you are not required to give any set amount. But as you prepare your money plan on a monthly or quarterly basis, you can estimate an amount you would like to give every week. If you make a practice of planning how much you will give ahead of time, giving will be easier. I tend to be a bit methodical and usually estimate 1 percent (one-tenth of the tithe) toward giving. You may choose, but make sure to plan. However, my advice is not to be too rigid in your planning—leave room for more. Also be prepared and have an open heart to give more if the need arises.

DO YOU REALLY TRUST GOD?

Pause now and ask yourself these questions: Do I really trust God as my source? Do I love God and His people enough to express that love through giving? Do I express my faith in God through giving?

I have discussed the importance of truly recognizing God as the source of all our needs, but it is paramount that we really connect to this truth. Knowing God in this way will help us to give freely because we will know for certain that He is able and available to help us at all times and provide for us.

Please pause and seriously ponder these questions. Let the Holy Spirit search your heart and show you where you stand as it relates to giving. He will let you know if you're withholding more than is right or if you're a generous giver. Ask the Lord to help you to be like Him—a loving giver.

Start Giving Now

Start giving. No matter how small the amount may be, commit to give on a regular basis to a charity of your choice, to your local church mission, or even to a child-sponsorship program. To ensure you do, set up a preauthorized payment plan. Watch and see how blessed you will be just by knowing you're making a difference in someone else's life. Your giving to someone has eternal value.

CHAPTER 9

Debt:
A Hangman's Noose for Many

Most households carry some form of consumer debt—credit cards and mortgages are the norm in most people's lives. People are consumer driven and convinced that whatever they want they must have now. This 'instant' or 'fastfood' society, along with relatively easy access to credit, has produced people who are so hungry for things that they are willing to go into debt just to have whatever they want. Until they come close to losing their property and dignity, many are willing to continue down this spiral of debt. Sadly, when they realize the debt is great, it seems almost too late in the game to change. But they can. They must seek to align their lives to God's will and work at being lenders rather than borrowers.

The rich rules over the poor, and the borrower is servant to the lender.

—Proverbs 22:7

For the Lord your God will bless you just as He promised you; you shall lend to many nations, but you shall not borrow; you shall reign over many nations, but they shall not reign over you.

—Deuteronomy 15:6

THE EFFECT OF DEBT

We are a consumer-driven society supported by hungry and willing credit card companies. Revolving credit coupled with revolving interest results in debt that takes long to repay. This world is burdened by debt, and in the body of Christ consumer debt has become a friend. But if you look carefully, you'll clearly see that easy access to other people's money for the purpose of buying non-investment type goods does more harm than good. You may get what you want right away, but you will pay the price for it later. You are often paying off debt for something you no longer have and that has not given you any positive rate of return.

Bad debt is the result of a bad habit—the habit of spending more than we earn. We spend other people's money at a high price. Consumer debt is the type of debt we need to avoid at all cost. This type of debt seems appealing—we get what we want more quickly. Unfortunately, it comes with a price—high interest and constant payments for items often no longer in use (they have been consumed).

Incurring bad debt is like gambling with your livelihood; you can't afford to play this way, and you are likely to lose. Ridding yourself of consumer debt is like an uphill battle, and this consumer debt comes with many drawbacks to you and your household.

Debt Enslaves

Debt is a hard taskmaster. When you are in debt, a merciless taskmaster rules you. No matter how gifted or educated you are, you are at the mercy of the man or organization you owe money to. You see no relief. You have no freedom, and the time you have belongs not to you but to the taskmaster you must repay. You wake up early to go to your job, not because you like it, but because you have bills to pay. Yet you cannot see any glimpse of hope because the little payment you make is eaten up by the charged interest. So your next option is to consolidate your debt, and for a little while you think you have the debt under control. But within months you see that you are back where you started—or worse. Often the problem is not with the inability to make the payments on time, but with your undisciplined tendency to keep charging more to credit cards. You create the cycle of debt all on your own.

Some people can't imagine life without credit cards—to live on a cash-only basis would be devastating to their standard of living. But how can you become debt free if you want to maintain your current level of living using debt? It doesn't work that way. Your aim should be to live debt free. Others have done it, so it is possible, and certainly with God on your side, you are more than able.

Debt Destroys Your Voice and Purpose

Slaves have no voice. Their master owns them to do his bidding. They cannot do what they please. They cannot speak as they wish. Their dreams have no hope of becoming reality.

Perhaps debt pins you down to a job you don't like. You get up each day, dreading your day, but you go to work because you have bills to pay and other responsibilities to take care of. Many would say that if they didn't have the debt, they would do something else or live somewhere else. The voices of many are silenced in the workplace; to speak up about what matters can be detrimental—the loss of a job needed to pay the bills.

Debt not only enslaves you, but destroys your vision and purpose. It limits you by killing your vision and destroying any hope you have. Why? Limited funds result in limited progress—in education, in business, in social standing, or in propelling you towards any dream you want to achieve. Yes, money answers all things. Without it your progress toward your life's dreams can regress, stagnate, or be brought to a halt because of lack of funds and heavy debt. If you have more than enough, you can do the things you want to do for yourself, your family, and others. God wants you to bless others. Maybe you can obtain higher education, start to invest in a business, or support a charity such as a medical research center or children's hospital. With debt hanging over your head, however, doing any good or fulfilling your life's goals or purpose is difficult without frustration or setbacks.

Debt Reduces Your Purchasing Power

Your cash flow is limited or lost when you are in debt. Why? You have bills to pay, plus your credit card debt to reduce. Generally you have little or nothing left to save or little extra cash for needs that may arise. You are embarrassed when some unexpected emergency requires cash, but you have none available.

Maybe you are unprepared for the unexpected. Perhaps debt restricts your ability to handle the unexpected.

Limited cash flow or no cash flow also causes you to lose out on great opportunities. You are unable to seize opportunities that are available only to the person who has ready cash. How often have you been presented with a business opportunity you really wanted to invest in but couldn't because of lack of funds? How many times have you lost out on the opportunity to give to a worthy cause? The opportunities that have passed your way are too numerous to count. Yet you continue to live a debt-ridden life and accept life as it is instead of seeking to change.

When you are free from bad debt, you are free to pursue your goals and able to "give toward every good work" or invest in good opportunities as they become available to you. Aim to be debt free. When you are debt free, you have freedom for you and your family; you have more cash flow, and when opportunities come along, you can invest in them wisely.

Debt Causes You to Feel Boxed In and Depressed

At times in my life, I have experienced lack, and it has never been a delightful experience. Most who are in debt and live from paycheck to paycheck can identify with similar thoughts. When you live from paycheck to paycheck, you feel like you're imprisoned and have no room to breathe. You pay the bills, but not much is left over to do anything extra. If an emergency arises—God forbid—and money is required, you are lost as to how to handle it. Sometimes if you have savings, you have to take from them just to cover expenses. Even going out for tea or coffee, or giving your child a treat, seems to be more like a problem or burden than a pleasure. In your mind you ask yourself if you should spend anything extra, even if it's only a dollar or five dollars. Living this way sometimes means you go without any cash in your purse or wallet because you have no extra to spare. The condition makes you sometimes wonder if God sees what's going on in your life.

This may sound familiar for most of you reading this. When in debt, you always owe someone other than yourself. You are obligated to pay that person or company until the debt is cleared. For many the debt is so much and never seems to go away. Why? Debt plus all the other obligations or responsibilities you have seem to limit you to paying only the minimum required amount. Sometimes you may even find yourself using that credit card or overdraft limit you vowed never to use because your commitments are more than what you earn. As such the debt stubbornly remains. Debt not only limits you financially, but also crushes you emotionally. The debt you owe makes you feel boxed in, with seemingly little or no hope of relief.

But a solution exists. The Lord sees your debt situation and knows creditors constantly knock at your door, asking for payments you cannot seem to make. But in His Word, He has given a solution.

Debt Destroys Relationships

The Word of God cautions us not to be surety for others because of the added responsibility we place on ourselves to take on someone else's debt should he or she default (Proverbs 6:1-5).

Although most know this very well, many still find themselves trapped in someone else's debt. How is this?

We may not go to the bank and finance company to sign on behalf of a friend or family member as surety, but we may find ourselves giving a small loan to someone to help him or her out. With a good heart and the hope that we are doing well, we lend only to face disappointment when repayment is not fulfilled. Then we are bruised emotionally and financially. A relationship is destroyed because our friend is unable to repay the money and doesn't know how to tell us—so he or she makes many excuses to avoid embarrassment or confrontation.

Good intentions do not always lead to good results. If you find yourself in a situation like this, you are better off not giving or giving just what you can as a gift and not as a loan. Too often, when situations like this occur among family and church members, good-hearted people are bruised.

Before I get to the solution, I encourage all of us to ask the Lord for forgiveness when we have failed to rely on Him and have depended on creditors and our own wisdom. We should ask the Lord to forgive our debt and give us wisdom to get out of debt because His will is for us to live debt free. We should also pray for favor with our creditors as we work to clear the debt we owe. Now let's see how the Word of God can provide the solution to our debt problems.

GOD'S DEBT SOLUTION

A certain woman of the wives of the sons of the prophets cried out to Elisha, saying, "Your servant my husband is dead, and you know that your servant feared the Lord. And the creditor is coming to take my two sons to be his slaves." So Elisha said to her, "What shall I do for you? Tell me, what do you have in the house?" And she said, "Your maidservant has nothing in the house but a jar of oil." Then he said, "Go, borrow vessels from everywhere, from all your neighbors—empty vessels; do not gather just a few. And when you have come in, you shall shut the door behind you and your sons; then pour it into all those vessels, and set aside the full ones." So she went from him and shut the door behind her and her sons, who brought the vessels to her; and she poured it out. Now it came to pass, when the vessels were full, that she said to her son, "Bring me another vessel." And he said to her, "There is not another vessel." So the oil ceased. Then she came and told the man of God. And he said, "Go, sell the oil and pay your debt; and you and your sons live on the rest."

—2 Kings 4:1–7

This story is quite familiar to many of us. We have heard many sermons preached and lessons taught on this passage before. Let us delve into the Word to see what God has to say about getting out of debt.

This woman and her husband were believers, but they were in debt. In many Christian households today, debt has taken up residence. Unfortunately, the husband died, leaving no inheritance but debt.

Many Christians are in the same boat as this family. Many leave their loved ones with debt rather than an inheritance. Loved ones find not so much as an insurance policy to cover funeral expenses! Yet these Christians call themselves righteous. If we are such righteous people, we should leave our families without the burden of debt in the midst of grief. We should leave a blessing to help them through the remaining years of their lives.

Debt enslaves. The creditors were about to take this woman's sons prisoners for life. Many of us are imprisoned by our own debt. We are slaves to the lender with no apparent way of release or escape. But God has a way out. What we will discuss is just one of His powerful ways to release us from debt's enslavement.

I like this woman; she went not to the prominent men of the day for advice, but to the prophet of God. She went to her godly leader and made certain he knew she was of the household of faith. She went where she believed she could get sound advice and practical help.

Seeking the help of a financial advisor or even a friend who is knowledgeable in financial matters would be prudent, but we find higher wisdom in the house of God. Although professional advice has its merit, we should also seek wise counsel in the body of Christ. While we should talk to our pastors, teachers, and deacons in the household of faith, of course we should talk to God for direction (Prov. 11:14; 15:22).

Based on the prophet's initial response, we can deduce that he seemingly didn't know how he could help. But his question is one we should ask: "What do you have in your house?" In other words, What do you have? What items can you sell? What can you give away? What do you not use that can be sold for cash? Let's look at this question another way. What do you have—gifts, talents, education, hobbies, or interests that can be turned into a product or service someone will gladly pay you for?

We often overlook or underestimate what we have. This woman said she had "nothing in the house but a jar of oil." What is oil? What does oil represent? Oil is as precious a commodity today as it was in biblical times. Everyone needs oil and has use for it. It is in high demand. We can find a market for it. No matter how high the price, we pay for it.

What 'oil' do you have in your house or in your life? What product or service can you render that people would be willing to pay for? Oil represents that high-demand product or service people will pay for. You must have something in you—a skill, gift, or expertise—people are willing to pay for.

For years I saw myself as only a financial services administrator. I tried thinking of ways I could earn extra income, and all I could come up with was bookkeeping, which was what I was already doing. But was that all I could do? Of course not. It took some soul digging, research, trials and errors to uncover the hidden values in my life. (Notice I called them 'hidden.' Sometimes we get so used to doing the same tasks for years that we cannot see ourselves doing anything else, and our hearts become veiled to the real us.) For years I researched something I could do that fit into my already busy schedule and that would work not only for me but also for my family. I wanted something that wouldn't take me outside my home more than I already was. With these requirements in mind, it took time, but I came up with one idea that was so simple and obvious yet hidden.

Often we sit in our acre of diamonds and don't realize it. My bookkeeping idea began to develop into something different and more in line with my interest. I learned that my love for reading and my keen attention to detail (I'm quick to spot errors and inconsistencies) were skills I could be paid to use. For me that realization was a revelation—not that I wasn't aware that others did this type of work for a living—that I could actually do it and love doing it. I also learned about my love for writing—I write journals, I take notes of almost every sermon at church, and this book and other articles are the result of my love for writing. As I learned what the "oil" was in my life and started doing research to learn how I could use these skills to help me, the Lord furnished the knowledge and ideas I needed on how to use that gained knowledge. Out of this researching and looking at what I had in my house, I now have a few business ideas, and the Lord has given me the business name for each of those ideas. Isn't God good?

In other words, don't think you have nothing. You can't be in Christ and have nothing. You were created in the image of God, and since you are like Him, then you have more than you think you do. If you are unable to come up with ideas on your own, ask God, friends, work colleagues and family members what you are great at doing. Take an inventory of your life, all you have done (not just work-related tasks), and what people say they appreciate you for. Sometimes you're too close the problem to see clearly or too stressed over the debt to see the possibilities. This woman thought she had nothing, but God showed her what she possessed. God will show you. If you lack wisdom, ask God for it. He is more than willing to give it to you (James 1:5).

Elisha's advice seems almost contrary. This woman was in debt, but he asked her to borrow vessels from her neighbors, probably the same neighbors who knew the debt load her husband had left her to deal with. I wouldn't advise more debt to get out of debt. Borrowing to pay off debt is just a vicious cycle and a disaster waiting to happen. The prophet's advice to borrow, however, was good. This type of borrowing involved making a business investment with an anticipated return. This type of borrowing was to be put into productive use—to make money, not to pay debt and still owe.

Why not just a few vessels? The more empty vessels, the more oil is poured out, and the more money or profit made. A few would limit the amount of income that could be made. The higher the production, the greater the return will be. For example, if you invest one hundred dollars for a guaranteed 10 percent return, in simple interest that would equate to ten dollars in profit. If you invest more, say one hundred thousand dollars, at the same rate of return, however, that would yield a higher amount, ten thousand dollars in profit. In this lady's case the more she borrowed, the more she produced, and the more income she received. Money brings money. Money put to productive, profitable use produces great returns.

Another beautiful analogy we can draw from this passage is that we should reproduce what we have. If a jar of oil fails to reproduce jars of oil, no profit has been made. That jar of oil represents our ideas that we can turn into wealth if we reproduce them many times over. We shouldn't settle for one idea. We should ask for many and reproduce them all.

We should take the advice of the prophet to heart. After we've borrowed our vessels—money and/or resources from others to help build our business—we should shut the door behind us and those working with us. We should avoid all distractions.

Notice, no neighbors were invited in—it was just the family, the ones who knew how dire the situation was. Sometimes we need to cut off the friend thing—going from place to place and eating out here and there—and focus on the need at hand. This may mean that we need to work late nights or early in the morning before going to our regular job. If we want to rise above this debt in our lives, we need to cut down on too much socializing—which only helps us spend more money than we need to and waste precious time. Often some friends can willingly help us spend our hard-earned money with all those get-togethers. The time comes when we need to work with our families and create an additional income stream to help pay off our debt.

The jar of oil, a miracle indeed, kept going until all the vessels were filled. The flow of ideas that bring wealth will keep coming until you say stop or become saturated. Don't settle for little. Aim high. God is ready to pour out His anointing to give wealth to you so you will be blessed and become a blessing to others. Ask God to keep the oil—the ideas, gifts, talents you thought were nothing—flowing so you can create more products or services that would benefit you, your household, and others. Ask Him to help you receive the ideas and use them as the oil keeps flowing.

Now, after you have produced all you can, be like this lady—go back for more advice. Ask God what your next step should be. Seek wise counsel. Take the advice the prophet gave: "Go, sell the oil and pay your debt; and you and your sons live on the rest." Sell your products or services, pay off your debt, and you and your family will live debt free on the extra money. There, the problem of debt has been solved. However, be careful to do this one thing first. Use the increase to pay off your debt. Then you can live on the rest. You should neither splurge the rest nor rack up more debt. From this point on, you should be debt free.

This formula is well suited for those who want to be debt free:

* Make up your mind to become debt free. Set a debt-free date.
* Seek advice from the wise.
* Examine what you have. Refuse to discount anything you have or do.
* Borrow only if needed to invest in your business or education. Borrow money or resources, ideas, and knowledge.
* Be focused on creating your product or service. Avoid distractions.
* Get support. Involve your family in the business.
* Ask for more oil from God. Ask for ideas to develop. Don't stop at one idea.
* Sell your products or services.
* Form the habit of saving and paying off your debt. The more you reduce your debt, the higher your net worth becomes.
* Live debt free on the rest. Live on a cash-only basis. Live a debt-free life.

God has placed in you and your life something you can use to help get out of debt and provide for the remainder of your life. God has provided more than enough to take care of you not only for today and tomorrow, but also for all your life and future generations. It's time to use your oil and get out of debt.

As you work toward living debt free, you will discover a new-found freedom. With your debt-free day approaching, your eyes will be opened to see not necessarily new opportunities, but opportunities that have been there all along. Recognizing your oil or the acre of diamonds you've been sitting on will give you a new drive to become free from debt. But being debt free comes with the responsibility to be a blessing. This new way of living makes it possible for you to be no longer a borrower but a lender to many.

Debt Tip

Debt can have a cloudy, dismal effect on your mind; at times you cannot see beyond the mountain of debt. Before you can get out, you must first see yourself being debt free. Every day spend fifteen minutes dreaming about what life would be like for you and your family without the debt burden. Thank God for setting you free from debt. Start asking yourself as well as your family, friends, and God what you have that you can use to make extra income. As you get ideas, act on them and see what the Lord will do as you take these steps of faith.

CHAPTER 10

Lend:
You Should Be on This Side of the Fence

Why are many so in debt that they can't even loan someone one hundred dollars? Why would God say that you should lend and not borrow? Christians should be the ones facilitating the building of schools and hospitals, funding other worthy causes, paving roads, and creating financial institutions. In other words, Christians should provide social care to society, thus demonstrating the love of God. Yet many people do not know your God who does these things. You need to get back to God and His path and be a lender to the nations (the unrighteous), not a borrower. How else will others know the greatness of your God if you are always on the borrowing side?

The Lord will open to you His good treasure, the heavens, to give the rain to your land in its season, and to bless all the work of your hand. You shall lend to many nations, but you shall not borrow.

—Deuteronomy 28:12

A good man deals graciously and lends; he will guide his affairs with discretion.

—Psalm 112:5

WHY ARE YOU NOT A LENDER?

Are you a lender? Maybe not or maybe you do, but not as much or as often as you would like. Many Christians are generally not in a financial position to lend because they do not have. They are constantly borrowing. Disobedience to God in any area can result in financial lack. Throughout this book, we have identified several reasons for financial problems. In summation, the main reason is that we are conducting our affairs as we see fit and not doing things God's way.

The Old Testament gives many examples of how the Israelites fell into sin. Each time the consequences of their sin were debt and enslavement to other nations. When they recognized and confessed their faults, God in His mercy lifted them up and restored them.

You too need to recognize where you have fallen

and confess your sin—whether it is related to how you manage your finances or to other areas of your life. Seek God's mercy to lift you up out of debt and into abundance. God wants to make you the head, not the tail. He wants to place you above others and give you the ability to lend to others instead of borrowing from them. By being a lender, you help someone in need and become a blessing. So why then are you not in a financial position to lend?

Lack of Obedience to God's Word

When you disobey God's Word, the results can lead to devastation. Instead of being in the strong financial position of being a lender, the results of disobedience are poverty, lack, and constant borrowing. Disobedience leads to being in a position you may think is hopeless.

When you obey God's commands and walk in His will, His promise is this: "The Lord will open to you His good treasure, the heavens, to give the rain to your land in its season, and to bless all the work of your hand. You shall lend to many nations, but you shall not borrow" (Deut. 28:12). In other words, the Lord will rain His blessings (including financial blessings) on you and your life as you need them, and He will cause your work to prosper. Furthermore, this blessing will lift you up and enable you to bless others through lending, and you will have no need to borrow from anyone.

Just as God will gladly overtake you with His blessings because of obedience to His Word, however, you can experience an opposite result when you disobey Him. Curses come to overtake, confuse, and destroy your life when you disobey the Lord. God clearly states in Deuteronomy 28:43–44, "The alien who is among you shall rise higher and higher above you, and you shall come down lower and lower. He shall lend to you, but you shall not lend to him; he shall be the head, and you shall be the tail." The results of disobedience are devastatingly manifold and rather unpleasant even to read. Often you want to know the blessings, but ought to be fully aware of the consequences of disobedience.

Have you examined your life lately? What is the reason for your dire financial situation? Does it have anything to do with poor money management? God wants you to be a good steward of the resources He gives to you. Do you work hard, tithe, give, save, and do all the right things financially but still struggle? Maybe you should consider other areas of your life. What about your relationships? Are you harboring lack of forgiveness or resentment in your heart? Your inability to stand strong financially may not always directly relate to how you manage your money, but to other areas of your life. Pause now and ask the Holy Spirit to show you whether you are doing or not doing something that is causing financial lack and therefore preventing your ability to lend to others.

Blessings come to those who follow God's way, and one such blessing is the ability to lend to others rather than to borrow from them.

Burdened with Debt

One of the limitations debt places on us is the inability to lend help to someone in need. We know that without money, opportunities to give, invest, or lend to someone in need will be out of reach. Many desire to do the good work of giving or lending to others, but this is only a desire. Why? After paying the bills and meeting basic needs, they have no extra to give or lend to anyone. Yet the Word of God says that when we give, the Lord will make grace abound toward us so we can have more than enough for every good work (2 Cor. 9:8).

If lending is a good work, then why don't you do it? Are you giving joyfully, cheerfully, and willingly enough so God can ensure you have more than enough to bless others? Maybe you miss the mark of being in a lending position, not because you give but because you are overburdened with debt. In some cases, you may lack enough funds to lend a helping hand to anyone, much less take care of your own basis needs. Why? You have more of the month to go than you have money to take care of your living expenses and financial obligations. Instead of being a lender, you are burdened by debt or repeating debt cycles.

God desires to provide you with more than enough, but how can He when you willingly enslave yourself to others through debt and fail to trust Him to meet your needs? How can God bless you when you have no plans to get out of debt, but rather appear content to stay in it? If debt is a mark of your financial mismanagement, how can God trust you with more?

If you desire to be a lender, then take first steps toward becoming debt free. Ask for God's forgiveness, seek His wisdom, and make a plan to remove the debt and live completely under the care of the Master. With Him on your side, you will eventually become a lender and not a borrower.

Can God Trust You?

If God should bless you with more than enough, can you be trusted? Can He trust you to manage the blessing well as a good steward? Can God trust you to be fair to others when you are able to lend to them? Or will you abuse your financial position?

As a means of aid to others, God instructs you to lend to others freely, as shown in Deuteronomy 15:8. "But you shall open your hand wide to him and willingly lend him sufficient for his need, whatever he needs."

God always instructs us with good reason. He knows the condition of a man's heart. Sometimes we may start well by lending to someone who needs it, but as time passes we find ourselves holding a grudge against that person or acting abusively toward him or her. Let us see how the Jews treated their own when times of hardship arose.

> *Now the men and their wives raised a great outcry against their Jewish brothers. Some were saying, "We and your sons and daughters are numerous; in order for us to eat*

and stay alive, you must get grain." Others were saying, "We are mortgaging our fields, our vineyards and our homes to get grain during the famine." Still others were saying, "We have had to borrow money to pay the king's tax on your fields and vineyards. **Although we are of the same flesh and blood as our fellow Jews and though our children are as good as theirs, yet we have to subject our sons and daughters to slavery. Some of our daughters have already been enslaved, but we are powerless, because our fields and our vineyards belong to others."** *When I heard their outcry and these charges, I was very angry. I pondered them in my mind and then accused the nobles and officials. I told them, "You are charging your own people interest!" So I called together a large meeting to deal with them and said: "As far as possible, we have bought back our fellow Jews who were sold to the Gentiles. Now you are selling your own people, only for them to be sold back to us!" They kept quiet, because they could find nothing to say.*

So I continued, "What you are doing is not right. Shouldn't you walk in the fear of our God to avoid the reproach of our Gentile enemies? I and my brothers and my men are also lending the people money and grain. But let us stop charging interest! Give back to them immediately their fields, vineyards, olive groves and houses, and also the interest you are charging them—one percent of the money, grain, new wine and olive oil." "We will give it back," they said. "And we will not demand anything more from them. We will do as you say." Then I summoned the priests and made the nobles and officials take an oath to do what they had promised. I also shook out the folds of my robe and said, "In this way may God shake out of their house and possessions anyone who does not keep this promise. So may such a person be shaken out and emptied!" At this the whole assembly said, "Amen," and praised the Lord. And the people did as they had promised.

—Nehemiah 5:1–13 (NIV, emphasis added)

This Scripture speaks for itself. The excessive lending practices resulted in powerless people and slavery. Families—parents and children—were enslaved and had hardly enough to live on. This is not the type of lending God accepts. Scripture instructs us that when we lend to those in the household of faith, we should not charge interest as though we were a lending institution (Ex. 22:25).

In the marketplace, this type of advantageous lending practice has placed many families in financial crisis. Lending has been freely done, but at extremely high rates and for amounts most find difficult to repay. The loss of jobs and homes in many American states has left broken families who have little or no hope of financial recovery.

When you are in a financial position to lend to someone, how do you go about it? Do you do it willingly to help someone in need? Can God trust you to lend to others fairly? As a financial pillar in your family, church, or community, please represent God, your Father, well by being a gracious lender.

You Are Unwilling to Lend, Even If You Have

If there is among you a poor man of your brethren, within any of the gates in your land which the Lord your God is giving you, you shall not harden your heart nor shut your hand from your poor brother, but you shall open your hand wide to him and willingly lend him sufficient for his need, whatever he needs. Beware lest there be a wicked thought in your heart, saying, "The seventh year, the year of release, is at hand," and your eye be evil against your poor brother and you give him nothing, and he cry out to the Lord against you, and it become sin among you. You shall surely give to him, and your heart should not be grieved when you give to him, because for this thing the Lord your God will bless you in all your works and in all to which you put your hand. For the poor will never cease from the land; therefore I command you, saying, "You shall open your hand wide to your brother, to your poor and your needy, in your land."

—Deuteronomy 15:7–11

God in His great wisdom knows that in this fallen world are those who do not have enough and need help. He admonishes us to give or lend to those in need; God warns against thinking evil or being grievous when lending to someone. Yet many fall into the trap of being grumpy lenders or refuse to lend with graciousness, even if they have the resources available to do so. They fail to recognize that God is the One who rewards the good deeds of giving and lending to others in need. Somehow, a misconception exists that all their abundance is for their use alone and that they don't need to use some of it to be a blessing to others.

Jesus spoke from one good nugget of wisdom to another, and in Matthew 5:42, while saying we should go the extra mile when asked, told us to do something extra. We should be willing to lend to those who ask and not turn them away. "Give to him who asks you, and from him who wants to borrow from you do not turn away."

The wisdom teacher advises us to give when it is in our ability to do so. We can also apply this practice when we have enough to lend to others. Proverbs 3:27–28 says, "Do not withhold good from those to whom it is due, when it is in the power of your hand to do so. Do not say to your neighbor, 'Go, and come back, and tomorrow I will give it,' when you have it with you." Just as it is with giving, so it is with lending. When we have to give, we should give. When we have to lend, we should lend.

Why say this? Clearly, some have the ability to lend but are unwilling to do so. Often we are unwilling to lend to others because we doubt they can afford it and wonder if they will pay us back. We gain no credit to ourselves if we think and act like the world. Jesus Himself said,

> *But if you love those who love you, what credit is that to you? For even sinners love those who love them. And if you do good to those who do good to you, what credit is that to you? For even sinners do the same. And if you lend to those from whom you hope to receive back, what credit is that to you? For even sinners lend to sinners to receive as*

> *much back. But love your enemies, do good, and lend, hoping for nothing in return; and your reward will be great, and you will be sons of the Most High. For He is kind to the unthankful and evil. Therefore be merciful, just as your Father also is merciful.*

—Luke 6:32–36 (emphasis added)

Jesus expects us to lend without looking for repayment. Why? Because the Father will reward us for our good deed, and the reward He gives is greater than any loan we could make. Jesus promises us not only a great reward but also adoption into a family where our Father is the Most High, the Creator of the universe. That promise is certainly better than any repayment we could receive from a loan.

If you find yourself resistant to lending or giving, please ask the Lord to break that withholding spirit and free you to have a generous nature like His. Then, with this new freedom and in wisdom, lend when it is in your ability to do so. Lend without wishing for something in return, and God, your Father, will bless you!

You Lend to the Wrong People

Often in your willingness to help, you may lend to the wrong person. The wrong person may be someone who is always borrowing and has a reputation for not repaying. In this case, let the lender beware. Be cautious of those who are always asking for a loan from friends and family members with promises to repay. Often the borrower usually fails to keep the promise. Lending to close relations and friends can sometimes prove to do more harm than good. If the lending transaction doesn't go well, it can result in broken relationships. In some cases, you as the lender may try to usurp authority over the borrower because you see yourself in a higher position. When you lord over someone else, the demonstration of love you initially intended is tarnished, and continuing the relationship as before becomes difficult. If the borrower fails to repay on time or cannot repay at all, you, the lender, may become disillusioned about the person's character or integrity. You may not want to continue the relationship further because you are unsure that person can be trusted anymore.

As a teenager, I sometimes had enough to lend to my siblings. I never thought much of it. I found great pleasure lending to them—I was helping them out. Unfortunately, I thought everyone was the same. When I was older and had a full-time job, a family member asked me for loan. Not being the type to refuse when I have means at my disposal, I lent this money, thinking as usual that it would be repaid—as in times past with my siblings.

Unfortunately, the repayment never happened. Initially, I was disappointed, but this situation taught me a few lessons. First, I forgave that person and moved on. I recognized that not everyone is honest in handling money matters. Jesus said to lend, never expecting anything in return (Luke 6:35). Just give the money away, especially when in your heart you are unsure whether the person will repay. To be able to lend to someone, knowing you are helping, is a great blessing. It gives the lender joy and the borrower temporary relief. Be wise, however, in your lending.

BENEFITS OF LENDING

So, what position do you find yourself in—are you a lender or a borrower? Do you have more than enough to bless others, or do you need a blessing? Are you the head and not the tail, or are you above and not beneath? Are you debt free, or are you in too much debt to help anyone? God wants to bring you into abundance so you can bless others through lending. He wants you to be the lender and not the borrower. But what are the benefits to being a lender?

Personally, you would feel good knowing you are able to help someone out temporarily. Even though you are providing them short-term relief, you have a sense of peace and even accomplishment as you help them solve a problem. The person who receives your help is also grateful for it.

From a business perspective, you become part of the solution and not the problem when you lend to companies that need cash flow to operate or make improvements to their businesses. Business lending benefits not only the organization that borrows but also the lender who earns interest on the loan. This type of transaction is usually mutually beneficial to both parties. A lending transaction usually brings a positive rate of return to both parties.

Apart from the personal inward pleasure and financial benefits to being a lender, the ultimate benefit to lending is the blessing of what no money can buy or no repayment can cover. When you lend to the less fortunate or poor, the Lord promises to bless you in all your work and in everything you do. Do you understand that? God will bless everything you do—as a mother, father, employee, business owner, investor, minister of the gospel, and a student. Yes, whatever you do, God will bless. He guarantees prosperity, all-around success, when you willingly lend to those in need. This is a blessing no money can buy. (Deut. 15:10).

Although lending has benefits, you must take care to follow God's will in doing so. Not everyone is in a position to lend, but those who can and do should allow God's Word to be the guiding lamp in the process. So what does it take to be a lender?

WHAT IT TAKES TO BE A LENDER

A lender is a person or organization who gives temporary use of something on the condition that the same or the equivalent will be returned. Being a lender is based not only on your financial ability to extend loans to others, but also on the responsibility to know who to lend to, what to lend, and how to handle the lending process. God in His wisdom knew that poor people would always be among us. He also knew about those who have more than enough to lend to the poor. Your wise Father, therefore, laid down guidelines throughout His Word about how the lending process should be handled.

So who do we lend to? In Deuteronomy 15, God instructs us to willingly lend to the poor. He specifically requested that we lend to the poor, to our needy brother or sister (in the body of Christ). God warned against being hard-hearted or tightfisted about lending to such persons (Deut. 15:7–9). To withhold when we possess it is sin in the eyes of the Lord.

As a lender, the borrower is under your control—he or she is obligated to repay the loan usually with interest and within a stipulated time. Be merciful to those to whom you lend. Avoid becoming puffed up because of the position you hold. Lend with compassion and willingness, and the Lord will bless you.

Keep in mind that when you lend to the poor, you are lending to the Lord (Prov. 19:17), and the Lord Himself will repay you. Being in such a position, you probably don't need financial repayment, but certainly you have a need only the Lord can meet. Maybe you need healing or need to see some members of your family come to the Lord—whatever the need, the Lord can fill it. As you lend to the Lord, He can and will repay with greater returns than money can bring.

Lending to the poor within the body of Christ

comes with another instruction from God: Don't charge interest (Ex. 22:25–27; Lev. 25:35–43). This stipulation may be a hard one to take considering the difficult times in which you live. No one wants to be in a lending transaction in which he or she loses out financially. Yet God says if you are lending to a poor brother or sister in the Lord or even to a blood relative, you shouldn't charge interest. The person is already in a difficult position if he or she must borrow from you. To add fire to the pan, so to speak, only makes repaying more difficult for him or her. God wants you to show compassion and mercy as He would to him or her. You are Christ's representative on earth. Do as He would do and lend with mercy—not to enslave but to help.

Sometimes, however, you may at your discretion charge interest to those outside the body of Christ as a business transaction (Deut. 23:19–20). But when lending to those outside the family, you still need to be merciful. Jesus said that if you lend to your enemies, you shouldn't expect payment back, but be merciful to them. "And if you lend to those from whom you hope to receive back, what credit is that to you? For even sinners lend to sinners to receive as much back. But love your enemies, do good, and lend, hoping for nothing in return; and your reward will be great, and you will be sons of the Most High. God is kind even to the unthankful and evil. Therefore be merciful, just as your Father also is merciful" (Luke 6:34–36). You can lend as an act of mercy.

Lending in the way God instructs is an act of

obedience to Him. It shows that you love Him and trust Him as your source. Obedience to God results in no poor being among us (in the body of Christ), no debt, and no enslavement.

> *Of a foreigner you may require it; but you shall give up your claim to what is owed by your brother, except when there may be no poor among you; for the Lord will greatly bless you in the land which the Lord your God is giving you to possess as an inheritance—only if you carefully obey the voice of the Lord your God, to observe with care all these commandments which I command you today. For the Lord your God will bless you just as He promised you; you shall lend to many nations, but you shall not borrow; you shall reign over many nations, but they shall not reign over you.* (Deut. 15:3–6)

Lending Tip

You are righteous before God the moment you accept Christ as your Savior and Lord. Those around you, however, see your righteousness in your character and the good works you do. Lending is one such good work. Lend as an act of mercy or kindness rather than for business purposes alone. As you do, God will bless you and your children (Ps. 37:26).

CHAPTER 11

Plan:
Know What Your Money Is Doing
and Should Do

> *God said in His Word that He knows the plans He has for us (Jer. 29:11). The fact is, God is a planner and a very detailed one at that. If we are made in His image, planning, organizing, setting goals, and working those plans should be part of our internal makeup. We must realign our thoughts and ways to His. Money planning affects all other areas of life—it should be part of our whole life plan.*

For I know the thoughts that I think toward you, says the Lord, thoughts of peace and not of evil, to give you a future and a hope.

—Jeremiah 29:11

SO WHAT'S YOUR PLAN?

Planning and writing down our plans greatly enhances our chance of achieving them. Those who plan achieve their goals, but those who fail to plan usually fail to achieve anything they want. Even if they have some dreams of what they want to do in life, failure to plan and act on their plans ends in unfulfilled dreams.

Have you ever listened to old people talk about what they used to do and what they wish they had done? They talk about the life they failed to plan and the dreams they failed to achieve. Often such people end up being miserable in their old age because they look back and realize the opportunities and time that have passed for them. Too many sadly fall into the category of those who fail to plan their lives.

We can look at very few in the body of Christ and see success written all over them. Those who are unhappy or unsuccessful in their lives often question the motives of the successful ones. But who are we to judge their success in life? We don't know their story—where they were and how they reached where they are now. If we asked them to tell their story, we would notice that, apart from faith in God, they dreamed big, wrote down their goals, and worked the plan until it became a living reality.

If we are in Christ, created and formed in the image

of our great God, we should be like Him in many ways. God never failed to plan anything. He planned the creation of the world and how His children would be provided for. He planned the design of Noah's ark with great detail. He planned the tabernacle—every detail of it (in fact, it's so detailed that Bible readers want to skip that part). He planned our redemption from sin. He planned our lives and how we should live out our days. He planned the second coming of Christ. God has a plan, a blueprint, for everything, and it's written for us in the Bible. The detail by which God plans is hard for the human mind to fathom. Just as God planned all these things, however, He expects us to plan our lives as well and seek His counsel to ensure we are in line with His will.

If you are not planning your life goals, including your money goals, you are setting yourself up for failure. If you are planning but fail to work the plan, then you are just frustrating yourself and wasting your time. When God planned, He put His plan into action. Whatever God said He would do, He has done.

So what about you? Do you have plans for your finances and your life as a whole? If not, it's time to start acting like a child of God. Write down your plans and work on them, even though doing so takes a while; you will succeed (Hab. 2:2–4).

PLANNING LIFE LIKE YOU'RE TAKING A TRIP

Whenever you get into your car, you have a destination in mind. You have either one place or several places you'd like to go. If you're going to a familiar place, maybe you've already mapped out in your mind how you will get to your destination. If you're unfamiliar with where you're going, you may either use a GPS or Google Maps, or ask for directions ahead of time to determine how to get to your destination.

Life is very much the same. You know (or should know) in your mind's eye where you want to go and how to get there. You should be able to clearly map out what routes, stops, or diversions you need to make along the way to get to your desired destinations in life. Planning your life, including your finances, involves doing different things at different times along your life journey to your desired goal. You should have a season and a reason for everything you do or don't do in your life.

When you're driving a car, you don't do everything all at once. For example, you don't turn left and turn right at the same time; you don't stop and accelerate at the same time. When you are driving, everything you do is for a specific time and reason. Along the way, you may have cars in front of you, and you may need to slow down or drive faster, depending on what's ahead of you en route to your destination.

Planning your life and living it out are pretty much the same thing. Sometimes you need to stop and assess your position before you can determine your next move. At other times you may be able to move full speed ahead with your plans as you easily accomplish your goals. Then you may need to slow down and take your time, working through certain aspects of your plan, especially when you are in unfamiliar territory. You may come to a point on the road where either a left or a right will take you to your destination; you need to choose. Either turn will take you where you want to go. The problem is that one route will take you there more quickly than the other, but another route may be more secure than the other. So you must act wisely and hope that the choice you make is the right one. Yet no matter how many stops, starts, slowdowns, or diversions you make, your destination is clear in your mind, and you get there. Just as you get into your car with a destination in mind, so you must have a life's destination you want to reach. The process you go through to reach your physical destination is similar to the one you use to reach your life's goals.

Along life's road, just like any ordinary road, traffic jams can hinder you from reaching your destination at the time you anticipated. Jams may cause you to divert a little and take a slightly different route than you originally planned, but still your focus is on reaching your destination. Although your plans may be delayed, you should still keep your destination in mind. It is never too late to reach a long-anticipated dream. Focus on your goals despite the delays.

Whenever I get into my car in the morning to drive to work, I listen to the traffic news at least once before I get on the highway. This news helps me determine whether the route I'm planning to take is a good one. You should do the same thing with your life when you make your plans; you should listen to the One above to find out how the 'traffic' really looks. This would help you avoid too many traffic jams along the way. Maybe you make your plans and set about doing them without consulting God. When you plan, however, you should seek wise counsel for direction. God has a better view of your life (from above) than you do, and He knows the roads you can avoid. If you consult Him, He will direct you (Prov. 3:5–6). So my encouragement to you is to set your goals. Know that you will find obstacles along the way, but consult God to direct your paths.

WHY DO YOU FAIL TO PLAN?

Not Planning: 'I Don't Need To Plan'

You may have no idea what you want in life or perhaps you haven't thought about what you want. Thinking about it is too hard, or maybe you don't want to think about it at all. Studies show that an astounding ninety out of every one hundred people have no ideas or plans for their lives. The future for them is an open book. As some may say, "Whatever happens, happens." They drift along life's road without any specific aim in life and are often frustrated and bitter when they see others accomplishing their goals. Please, if this describes you, stop where you are now and begin to ask yourself some hard but very necessary questions. What do I want my life to look like over the next five years, the next ten years, or even the next fifty years?

Planning ahead for your life and finances gives you something to work towards each day. You have no guarantees that either will happen as perfectly planned, but your plans will happen once you overcome the obstacles and keep pressing toward your goals (Phil. 3:14).

Unbelief: 'My Goals Are Too Big'

Perhaps you don't believe that what you want to accomplish can happen. Maybe you've convinced yourself that you can't achieve anything. Sadly, you seem to lack faith in God to help you accomplish your plans. Sometimes I'm amazed at how many unbelievers accomplish such great feats in life, while believers who claim to serve a great big God cannot match them.

When you plan, believe in your plan and believe in your God to help you accomplish it. Look at your plans every day more than once—in the morning and at night (Hab. 2:2-4). The more you see your plans, painting mental and even visual pictures of your dream, the more likely you will achieve them. Remind yourself that you can do all this through Christ who gives you the ability to do it (Phil. 4:13). If you don't believe you can, you won't. If you believe you can, you will.

Fear of the Unknown:
'I Don't Want to Think about It'

Are you afraid of your financial future? Most people are afraid of their future—how they will live, how long they will live, if they will be able to take care of themselves financially without being a burden to others. Considering the news, you probably fear loss of income from your job or business, or whether your business will be profitable for years to come. The circumstances around you are enough to cause fear, not to mention your own inner turmoil about the future. As such, you'd rather not think about the future.

No one but God knows what tomorrow holds. But as a believer you should be comforted, knowing that the One who feeds the sparrow and numbered each hair on your head is the One who knows what tomorrow holds (Matt. 6:25–33). Furthermore, God has promised that everything (good or bad) will work out for your benefit (Rom. 8:28).

Laziness: 'It's Too Much Work'

Do you think planning is too much hard work? Maybe you feel based on your dreams that thinking, dreaming, and planning ahead demand too much effort. Furthermore, perhaps you think that working the plan is even more hassle than you need. Yet you long for the dream to come through. On the other hand you may do some dreaming and planning and even start, but along the way you may run into some setbacks or obstacles, or something happens that needs your undivided attention, so you drop the dream.

One thing about planning is that it requires constant effort and diligence. You must stick to your goal and be diligent and disciplined in the process. Sometimes you need to reorganize your plans because of setbacks or changes in your circumstances, but the key is to keep the goal in mind. Planning gives you focus. You need to keep working towards your dreams, even in the face of setbacks. Believing in what you are doing is also helpful. Remember the Word: "The plans of the diligent lead surely to plenty" (Prov. 21:5). Being diligent has its rewards: riches, authority, full satisfaction, profit, and more (Prov. 10:4; 12:24, 27; 13:4). Encourage yourself in the Lord to be diligent in your work.

Fear of Failure: 'I Don't Want My Efforts to Fail'

We are often afraid to dream big and plan big because we've already concluded that we will fail. We may have experienced failure in the past; the fear of failing again has caused us not to forge ahead and try again. It is true that sometimes we may fail at a business startup, exams, or some other goal. We may even fail, having tried the same thing several times.

But God doesn't want us to fail. We need to keep

this in mind when we are making our plans. God wants us to succeed. Over the years I have kept two things in mind that have helped keep me moving forward after failure. First, we must always remember that failure brings us one step closer to success. Successful sales people tell us that success doesn't happen overnight; they experience several negative responses before they get a positive one and make a sale. But they focus on the goal and remain persistent, knowing that every 'no' brings them one step closer to 'yes.'

Second, we must treat every failure, mistake, and setback as a learning tool. We should examine what went wrong and find out how we can make it work the next time. We should also seek the counsel of those around us who are wise and experienced in similar matters (Prov. 15:22). We should never let fear of failure be an excuse for not planning and moving full speed ahead when success awaits us.

Uncertainty about How to Start: 'I Don't Know How'

This is probably the greatest challenge when people plan their finances and family future. Trying to determine your financial position, projecting what you would like to achieve, and then planning your finances to get there, can be very daunting tasks. You may not have the temperament or inclination to take the time to review and file important documents, record your income and expenses, and plan how you will reach your goals. But the truth of the matter is, you can learn what you don't know how to do. Tons of books on personal finance are available. Different types of applications can help you get organized and stay that way. When it comes to the world of personal financial planning, your options are endless. If you don't want to learn, a knowledgeable and trusted friend or a financial professional can help you. What's important is not only acknowledging that you don't know how, but seeking help to overcome that limitation. If you don't know, ask. It doesn't hurt to ask for help; you gain the benefit of help and increased knowledge.

GOD PLANS, SO YOU SHOULD TOO

God is the greatest example of a planner. We have been created in the image and likeness of God, our Father. As such, God expects us to be like Him—a chip off the old block—and be planners. God plans and expects us to plan too.

God formed this world, and His plan to keep it functioning for our benefit unfolds before us every day. God planned for our salvation. Thousands of years passed for this plan to unfold, but Jesus came from heaven to earth and executed God's plan to die for our sins and rise in victory. God's plan is still unfolding before us every day, and we can see that times and seasons unfolding before us are leading to our Lord's return.

Personally, God has made plans concerning you—

your life and your family. Jeremiah 29:11 bears greatly in my mind that God's plans for you are good. Let your plans come to line up with His—they are good and give you a future and a hope. As you do, keep in mind that everything in God's plan is destined to work out for your benefit. Don't fail to plan and live in failure. Plan like your Father would with specifics and see your plans lead to profit.

Planning is a difficult task that requires discipline, but it is only one part of the process to accomplish your goals; you need to work on your plans. But do you have any plans to start with, or are you the wandering type, walking aimlessly through life without any thought of what your life should look like next year, in two years, in five years, or even in fifty years from now? Just as God took time to plan this world, your life, your salvation, and His return, so you should make plans for your life.

Take time to assess your life and ask God what His will is for you. Even with respect to your finances, God has a plan and He certainly desires that you prosper—physically, spiritually, financially, and relationally (3 John 1:2). For each person in the body of Christ, He has a blueprint of what He wants to do and how He wants each believer to prosper in life and finances. If you have failed to make a plan for your life up to this point, please start planning now and start setting goals for yourself. If you haven't dreamed yet, start dreaming—big dreams and not small ones. God has plans for you; ask Him to help you make them a reality in your life. Let those around you see the good plans God has ordained for your life. Let the prosperous life you live glorify God. To get there, start dreaming, start planning, keep planning, keep praying, and keep working your plans until you are living them out.

THE POWER OF PLANNING

Of course, planning takes time and effort. It takes some serious soul-searching, or so you may think. But planning is really only a written vision of what is already inside you. You have dreams and goals you would like to accomplish, and planning is merely the starting point to make all that is inside you become a reality outside of you. It is not a waste of time or energy. Planning is a powerful tool you need to make your dreams become reality. By planning your finances and life, you have much to gain.

Planning Obligates God to Work for You

No one wants to be unsuccessful in life. What form that success may take doesn't matter; the important thing is knowing what success looks like to us. We have a life dream for ourselves, for our families, for our finances, and for every area of our lives. We want to succeed, and as much as we want to succeed, God wants us to succeed all the more.

Christians often settle for whatever happens, but God doesn't. His unrelenting interest in our success is evident in how much planning and work went into our salvation, healing, deliverance, prosperity, and success. He willingly offered His only Son for your sake and mine so we would experience abundance and live eternally. Yet we often settle for whatever happens. Our success in life is a direct reflection on God—who He is.

When you make plans to fulfill your purpose in life according to God's will, you obligate God to come alongside you and make sure you succeed. Why? Your successes honor God. But struggling through life financially or in any way fails to bring God praise. Any failure in your life dishonors the name of God. Therefore, for the sake of His name, God will help you bring your plans to reality. When you succeed, not only will you and others praise and glorify God, but the success itself will be a monument of praise to God. Your success honors His name.

Planning Is Faith in Action

To achieve any success, you must have a plan. Hebrews 11:1 is the guidepost of what faith is. When you plan anything, you act in faith. Your plan says that you are sure of the things you hope for, and it is the evidence, the written proof, of things not yet seen. Your goals are the visions and dreams you have written in the here and now. Planning is the act of faith that gives you the ability to capture on paper what exists not yet physically, but inside you. Faith is what you see, not what others see. Faith is hoping in the dreams and visions God has placed inside you and seeing them in the here and now. Planning is taking the future and writing it on paper now. Whatever dream you have becomes possible when you put it on paper. Planning writes your future; it declares your destiny.

Furthermore, when you plan, you attract God's attention. Your plan speaks to God. Your plan says you have faith in God and are convinced that He will give you what He has promised.

Planning Obligates You to Act

You may have visions of grandeur and a great plan to accomplish them, but you may still fail. No plan is worth effort and time without a corresponding action. You must go beyond the planning stage. You may have good intentions or the habit of procrastination or the inclination to be downright lazy. None of these things will take the dream God has given you from paper to reality. You must plan your work and work your plan.

The purpose of planning is to help you put your visions into baby steps so you can run with them (Hab. 2:2-4). In other words, the plan provides a pathway to your success, and all you need to do is follow it. Yes, sometimes the pathway may seem like a long road to the end, but if you keep pressing on and doing what you need to do, you will succeed. The Lord said that though it may take a while, it will surely happen. Keep the plan, and sometimes rework the plan if needed, but stay focused on the prize, and you will win!

Planning Protects You

This statement may sound weird, but it's true. Planning preserves your life. When you plan, you say to yourself, to God, and to the world, "I'm not waiting for life to happen to me. I will make life the way I envision it to be." When you plan, you refuse to settle for whatever happens – you bring definition to your life. You make sound decisions based on your plans. You become true to the vision God has given you and you don't allow yourself accept life the way it is. You keep focused on your dream, not what is happening around you. The plans give you the push to keep moving and protect you from settling or wandering through life. Your vision keeps you from perishing and struggling in this life.

You're Not Alone

The wonderful fact of being a Christian is that you are not alone. Even in your planning process, God is with you. The beautiful thing about your future is that God has already written it on your heart—that is, in your mind. You may have dreams that seem so big and so out of the box that you don't share them with anyone. You don't voice them or plan them because they are too scary, yet you have a burning desire to do them. You have a burning desire to prosper in your finances, to upgrade your education, to do something you've always dreamed of. Proverbs 16:9 says, "A man's mind plans his way, but the Lord directs his steps." Your responsibility is to take those dreams and make plans (your first step of faith). Then, as you work out those plans, God will direct your steps and establish your plans. God's commitment to you is to make your plans become reality. Take that step, plan your life, plan your finances, and God will order your steps and make your dreams become reality.

KEEP TRACK OF YOUR MONEY

Often you may find you are in financial straits because of the poor financial choices you have made. Sometimes your bad daily financial habits—overspending, not living on a budget, and not monitoring your financial progress—may result in debt and lack. Other times a major decision you didn't give much thought, prayer, or proper research to may turn into a financial disaster.

Sometimes sickness of a major contributor to the family's income may cause difficulty, and in the midst of dealing with emotional and physical aspects of that person's care, you naturally overlook family finances. Then, before you can attend to your finances or fully rebound from these family matters, the financial situation becomes a burden. With pressing matters vying for your attention, perhaps neither you nor your family members took the time to review, assess, and adjust to the decreased income and/or increased living expenses that occurred because of the illness.

Untimely death or loss of a job may also bring unwanted financial challenges. Other matters such as divorce affect a new single parent's ability to adjust to one income and child support, if any—not to mention the emotional effects of the divorce itself. Whether you like it or not, you need to deal with such issues in this fallen world. You must therefore be prepared for such unexpected occurrences in life.

Examine Your Financial Position

How often do you review your finances and project for the future? Financial professionals advise conducting an annual review of your financial condition and position. You should compare your current financial position to your goals to determine whether you are closer to or further away from what you last projected. Even if you do not or cannot hire a financial planner to help you in this process, make it your business to be your own planner or ask a trusted friend to help you and make you accountable.

Set financial goals for yourself. In my opinion a year is too long to wait before doing a review. Too much can happen in a twelve-month time span. Catching an expense sooner will help you readjust and keep on track toward your main goal. In my opinion, you should do semi-annual or even quarterly reviews of your position and make any necessary adjustments to ensure you reach your goals. Life is hard work. Handle your life and your family's well-being as a business.

Manage the resources the Lord gives you in a business-like manner. As most successful businesses do:

* Prepare a budget. Project your income and expenses, such as major projects you need to finance (house, car, vacation, and so on);

* Develop a plan. Outline how you will reach your financial and other life goals;

* Work that plan. Act on the decisions you have made. This is the only way to bring them into reality. Use these projections as your daily guide to managing your money.

Review where you are now. Don't wait until trouble comes, but be proactive in your life and your finances.

Be scrupulous about your money—how you earn, tithe, save, give, invest, spend, borrow, or lend. You should know what your income and expenses will be at least ninety days in advance. Please don't tell me the numbers are in your head. Write them out; calculate ahead of time what you're doing with your money. Having a visual hard copy of what's happening will bring you into a full realization. Don't get caught off guard! Be financially prepared.

Consider My Simple Money-Management Process

At the beginning of each year, I create a running spreadsheet of my checking account and record projected income and expenses for the year. I try to stay within the parameters of those projected figures. My spreadsheet lets me know in advance what's coming my way. I record actual amounts as they occur and update any changes in projected amounts when they become known (e.g., increase of insurance rates). This practice has helped keep me out of troubled waters.

You can easily start this process by downloading a year's history from your online bank account. If you know where you spent your money, you can easily categorize each item, determine which excesses to eliminate, and continue with the good financial practices you have developed. These practices give you a global view of what's coming in and going out of your account and show whether you will be in a positive or negative position. You will also be amazed at how much actually passed through your hands in one year. Something else you may notice is that your cash withdrawals are just that—cash withdrawals. You don't know what you spent that money on.

I also use the spreadsheet to monitor my financial position (my assets less my liabilities) and help monitor where I am financially in contrast to where I want to be. The only drawback with the spreadsheet method is that I must enter the items manually when updating it. But the advantage of this practice is that I become keenly aware of how I am spending my money.

I like the spreadsheet format, but it may not appeal to you. As an alternative, you can use personal finance software to track your banking transactions—checking, savings, investments, credit cards, mortgages, lines of credit, and so on. Also, personal finance software can create reports on all account activity and categorize it into income and expense categories. Personal finance applications are rich with features that will help you budget and set financial goals. You can even prepare regular reports to chart your progress toward achieving these goals. These reports can help you determine whether you need to make improvements or are on track with your goals.

In addition, you can even use this software to manage your cash-only transactions. Keeping records of cash transactions, however, can be very time consuming. I did this for one year to determine what exactly I was spending my cash in hand on. You don't need to do this for a year, but you can keep a one-month record to see how you are spending this portion of your money. For each cash transaction, I receive a receipt so I can keep an accurate record of what happens to this cash. What you do with cash in hand will surprise you. Recently, to keep it simpler, I tried to limit the amount of cash withdrawals and use my bank card more. This makes the monitoring of my spending activity much easier.

Regardless of which method of financial management you choose, don't delay starting the process. No matter how much or how little you think you have, monitoring your financial activities is a good money management discipline.

STEPS TO YOUR FINANCIAL SUCCESS

So at what level are you in planning not only your finances, but all areas of your life? Do you have a plan for any area of your life, whether it is your spiritual walk, family, other relationships, health, career, or finances? If not, I ask you to please start. The only person who stands to lose from not planning your life is you. If you don't pause now and begin this process, no dream or goal you have will likely become reality. Remember, your plan gives birth to your dream.

So how can you begin planning your life and finances? Ask yourself a few starting questions and write down your answers:

* What do I like to do?

* What are my interests in life?

* What are my gifts, talents, and education; and how can I use them to be a blessing to others?

* What level of financial success do I want to have?

Answer these questions without questioning your answers. Just write down what instantly comes to mind. What you write will amaze or surprise you. The process will also feel quite liberating. Taking time to do this is critical because it will determine the level of success you achieve in your life and finances.

So much of what we want to do in life requires money. We need money for basics like food, clothing, and shelter. We need money for career development, a business startup, a dream vacation, regular giving to our church or a charitable work, and help for a friend. Regardless of what we do, money is one of the basic requirements to make it happen. We need to match our finances to our life purpose.

To help you begin that process of linking your goals to your finances, start by writing down all areas of your life that would benefit from planning. Set a goal of where you would like to be in those important areas of your life. Then, to get a clear picture of the gap between your desired goals and your current position, evaluate where you are in each of those areas right now. What steps do you need to take to close the gap between where you are now and where you want to be? Write them down. Create an action plan for each area of your life—the baby steps you need to take to reach your goal. Make an estimate or, better yet, do some research to understand the cost involved to reach each goal. In some cases the cost is just your effort and time (for example, a healthy life may require adding exercise to your routine but doesn't require money). In other cases an actual financial outlay is required—for example, if you're building your dream home or taking a much-needed dream vacation.

Now take time to gather into a binder all your financial information—bank statements, insurance records, investment account statements, mortgage and credit balances, car lease or purchase terms, and other pertinent details. Then calculate your financial position—how much you own less how much you owe. Make a money plan that includes your income and expenses. Remember to include your action steps for those goals not already included in the money plan. Go easy on yourself and start a money plan for at least ninety days ahead. You want to determine whether you have enough cash flow and plan ahead on which expenses you need to eliminate. By doing your money plan, you may realize you need to negotiate credit terms or find low rates for standard expenses such as housing, car insurance or other insurances, television, telephone, Internet, and transportation. Use the ninety-day money plan to examine your actual spending over that time period. Make necessary adjustments to your projection and start the ninety-day plan again. Along with monitoring your cash flow through the ninety-day money plan, you will also evaluate your financial progress. Are you getting closer to or further away from your financial and life goals?

Financial planning—in fact, any kind of planning— is ongoing and takes time. During the process you can learn a lot about yourself, and using your goals helps you to keep focused. Planning can also be a bit overwhelming, so enlist a friend or hire a financial planner or money coach to help you in the process. The objectivity or professional help will serve to guide and motivate you along the way. As you stay disciplined, you will indeed reap the rewards of financial empowerment to be a blessing to others.

Planning Tip

Not only does the power of planning or projection obligate you to act, but the Lord will also work with you on your behalf to achieve financial success. Start planning and work your plan today.

CHAPTER 12

Keys to Keep It All in Perspective

> *Getting caught up in the spirit of mammon is so easy. We can become driven and consumed by money—making it, spending it, and keeping it all for ourselves. God wants us to recognize the necessity of it, but not let it control us. We need to apply God's principles and keep money under control.*

Keep your heart with all diligence, for out of it spring the issues of life.

—Proverbs 4:23

IS MONEY CONTROLLING YOU?

A s you come to the close of this book, I hope you are beginning a new journey with the Lord regarding how you handle the resources He has given to you. If you have started to change your attitude toward money and God and made changes to how you handle your finances, you're off to a good start. Like any less-traveled road however, you will find humps, bumps, and roadblocks along the way. As such, you need to keep this money journey in proper perspective.

The Bible says a whole lot about money, wealth, and riches. It speaks of those who had lots of wealth because of God's blessing on their lives. Then we see the other side of the coin; Jesus and others like James warned about the control money can have on us. Money is such a powerful thing simply because we can use it to fulfill our basic needs for food, shelter, and clothing; and because we can use it to influence others. We need to guard our hearts and not let it control us.

Money can control those who lack enough of it. It controls us when we don't have enough of it, when we have more financial commitments than we have money.

You may work more than one job or take every opportunity to work overtime. In the process you may have little 'you time' or 'family time.' Maybe you think you need the money so desperately that you ignore your need for rest, relaxation, and time to take care of your body. Perhaps you even miss your much-needed time with God, whether through your private devotions or church attendance. Maybe you miss family gatherings and special events with your children because you need to bring in that extra dollar.

Another way money controls us is when we have so much that we hoard it. Maybe we become so paranoid about losing what we have that we guard it.

Perhaps you live in misery and are so miserly that you can't enjoy life. You don't dare use any of what you have for a little entertainment, nor do you bless someone without grumbling about it. The other extreme is to flaunt your money and use it to get what you want from others for your benefit. Maybe you are tempted to buy friends rather than make them. This type of control may even cause family members to fight among themselves about how to get your money, while you worry about how to protect it. Money can control those who possess it.

Yes, for those who have little or much, money can control. The control money can have on us displeases God and is in no way beneficial to us. This controlling spirit causes us to dishonor God in all areas of our lives and tempts us to omit paying our tithe or giving offerings because we think we lack enough. We fail to recognize money's control over us and have no care or consideration for others or the kingdom of God.

Our perspective on money determines whether we control it or it controls us. Although this book is about money, the emphasis is more about our attitude towards it and towards God who provides for all. Life is about striking a balance and not allowing any one thing to take control. Our first and foremost priority is to the kingdom of God. When dealing with our finances, we need to keep that in mind. Matthew 6:33 emphasizes this—seeking God and living uprightly before Him as our priority yet guarantees that God will supply all our needs since He knows everything we need even before we ask. As we go through the highs and lows of life, we need to let go and let God, not the money; be in control. He is well able to take care of us. Let us keep money in its rightful position—under our control with God's direction.

THE PROBLEM WITH MONEY

If we fail to keep it in its proper perspective, money or the spirit of mammon can control us. That is why the Word of God tells us that the love of money is the root of all evil (1 Timothy 6:10). The problem with money starts when someone 'falls in love' with it. God warns us not to allow money to control us and hinder our relationship with Him. He doesn't, however, condemn the wealthy for having money. What He condemns are the bad practices and negative heart attitudes some develop because they have riches. Because of their riches, some think they are greater and better than others. Sadly, some become blinded in their thinking. Because they have lots of money, they think they no longer need God.

Are you consumed with money or are you overly concerned about it? Are you like the man who wanted Jesus to order his brother to share the inheritance with him (Luke 12:13)? Whatever you do, please don't get greedy. Your life—now and in the future—is way more important than money or possessions. Your life consists of more than having lots of money, big houses, or classy cars. Jesus is more concerned about your character than your comfort. He is more concerned about your eternal life and your relationship with God than about your having the latest gadgets and comforts of life that quickly fade away.

When you've done it all and reached your financial goals in life or achieved a certain level of success, don't get trapped into hoarding money like the rich fool in the story did. This attitude leads only to false security. You may think you've got your future all set with more than enough years to come. Like the rich fool, you may think it's time to sit back, relax, eat, drink, and be merry. If you have this train of thought, your motive is selfish. You no longer have thoughts towards God or a desire to please Him. Consumed by money, you don't even think you need God anymore. This is the danger zone, a zone in which you can easily get caught off guard. Actually, you are closer to death than you may think (Luke 12:19–21). Why? You are no longer living in a right relationship with God. Money and possessions have become your lord rather than Jesus being your sovereign Lord.

But being rich in things instead of being rich toward God is meaningless. Why have it all and not have God? To gather up all you can, hoard it and never give to bless others is pointless. You can keep all you have, but the day will come when, no matter how much you have, you won't be able to take it with you.

So why keep it all for yourself? Why be rich in things but not rich toward God? Ultimately, the soul of man, not the money or possessions of man, is what God looks at. Now is the time to disconnect from money and possessions and connect with God.

Do you want to be rich in God?

MASTER YOUR MONEY

How do we keep money in its proper place? How can we be masters over money and not let it master us? Jesus offers an immediate solution to this money problem. We will examine this solution and others that will keep money where it belongs—with us as its masters.

Don't Worry

Jesus offers an immediate solution to the rich fool syndrome (Luke 12:22–34). Don't worry about your life. Sounds simple, doesn't it? But maybe the solution hasn't been so simple for you. Worry is a form of control whether you have loads of money or little. If you aren't careful, money worries can so easily creep in and take over your life.

Hoarding money and keeping close watch over all our possessions are signs of money anxiety. Jesus encourages us not to worry or be anxious about the cares of life. We shouldn't be constantly worried or overly occupied about what we will eat or wear. These concerns are just a very small fraction of our lives. As the saying goes, we have bigger fish to fry. Our lives are far more valuable than having food, clothing, houses, cars, or prestigious careers—or being successful entrepreneurs. We are more valuable than the birds God takes care to feed daily. In the grand scheme of life, we are of utmost importance to God.

Worry of any kind is futile. It says we don't trust God enough to provide for us. Worry exalts our problem above God and makes it bigger than it actually is—in fact, even bigger than God. This preoccupation with our problem—or what we think is a problem—is not good for us. Worry does nothing to benefit us and has been proven to negatively affect our health and well-being. From sleepless nights to stressful days, to stomach ulcers and various types of health issues, worry has been an enemy rather than a friend. As Jesus said, it adds no benefit whatsoever to our lives. By it we won't gain the ability to increase our height or add even a unit of time to our days. All worry does is take away from us—our good health, restful sleep, energy, happiness, contentment, peace, and every blessing God has in store for us.

Even the lilies of the field have the Creator God watching out for them. Think of it—the lilies are here today and gone tomorrow. They are not humans created in the image of God, yet He cares for them, and they are more beautifully arrayed than Solomon with his great riches.

If God takes such great care of nature, how much

more will He take care of you, His precious child? Instead of worrying about your needs or about how much money you have or don't have, put your faith in God. Don't be anxious or troubled—or even try to reason too much—over your financial situation or the other needs in your life. Better yet, be confident in knowing that God, your Father, knows what you need. He not only knows but He will provide them for you. Blessing you is indeed God's pleasure. Therefore, trust in Him, and He will meet you at the point of your need.

One more important key to banishing money anxiety is what Jesus added—give it up. Give money, give gifts—don't keep it all for yourself. Instead of being preoccupied with money and controlled by it, give it away. Yes, I know you have responsibilities, and so does Jesus. He is not asking you to be irresponsible, but to master your money. At every opportunity, give toward a good work—money, clothes, food, whatever the need may be. Give and help someone in need.

In so doing, your hold on money is broken, and you will find freedom to live without concern for your needs because you know the Father will take care of you. The thing you can freely give is the thing that has the least control over you. The beauty of giving is that it not only gives in a temporal sense, but also brings eternal dividends. As you give, you contribute to the kingdom of God. Your act of giving changes lives for Christ. Your giving brings praise and glory to God. It shows that your heart is for God and stores up eternal rewards for you in heaven. To break the money hold, do not worry. Trust

God, seek Him, and give to His kingdom. Then the treasure of heaven will be full of blessing for you now and in the life to come.

Give Thanks

Something about saying Thank You to God makes a difference when we are journeying through life. I'm not just talking about aimlessly saying thank you, but doing so with thoughtful and heartfelt appreciation to God. We need to be thankful not only to God, but also to those He has placed in our lives who've been a blessing, a help, and an encouragement—even those who have rubbed us the wrong way and made our lives difficult. We have so much to thank God for if we would just pause long enough to think about it (Selah!).

Give Him the credit that is due to Him alone.

Lord, I thank You for . . .

* The job I have but don't like that much—it is one of Your ways to meet my needs.

* The business ideas You've given me that are yet to become realities. They show me that You are the God of creativity working through me.

* The broken relationship that has broken my heart. You've repaired my heart and restored my love for that special one.

* That which is not working well. You have promised

that everything, whether good or bad, will work in my favor.

∗ Limited finances. Through this challenge, You have proved to me that You can make much out of little. You have gifted me with a heart of contentment.

∗ The blessings I have received from others. You have shown me that You will neither forsake me nor cause my children to be in need. You are my great provider and the source of all I need.

We will find that appreciating God and people has a way of relieving the burden, the weight that life's problems bring our way. During the hard times, we should make it a practice to thank the Lord every day regardless of how grim things in life look. Appreciation also forces us to see the good even in the midst of the bad. We begin to realize that things are not as bad as we thought they were. Sometimes giving thanks to God brings tears to my eyes, not just because it's hard to do (especially when I'm feeling low) but because I recognize how faithful He is to me. I've learned to give Him the praise that is so rightly His.

In the midst of losing something dear to you, something you think you need, thank God. Thank Him for the privilege of having had that blessing in the first place, and you'll find that moving on will be a lot easier. You may have lost a house either by default or by being forced to sell it for some reason. Thank God for the house and for the wonderful times you and your family and friends experienced while there. Thank Him for the furniture, the appliances, and anything the house represented to you. Then move on. He will provide an even better future.

So thanksgiving causes us to appreciate our lives. When we thank God for where we are and where we've been, we'll see Him take us to where we want to go. Though this journey will take time, we'll find that we're getting close to our dreams when we appreciate Him for what He has done and is doing. We just need to make a conscious effort to thank Him every day and be specific about what we're thanking Him for. Here are some other ideas that may help.

* Create a gratitude journal and note three things you can thank God for each day.

* Thank God for what He is doing in advance of what you would like Him to do.

* Verbalize your gratitude immediately. As you receive blessings or think of God's goodness, say a simple "Thank You, Jesus."

* Take every opportunity to share with friends, family and even the stranger how grateful you are to God for His goodness toward you.

It's not always the asking in prayer but the giving of thanks that touches the heart of God to bless you. Giving thanks to Him in advance shows your faith in Him to meet your needs or fulfill your heart's desires. Anyone you appreciate will have a soft heart towards you and be willing to do more just because you have shown your appreciation. It is the same with men as it is with God. Never fail to give thanks every day—to God and others.

Think Success

The road to financial wellness takes some time. The time it takes varies from person to person. But as you practice proper financial management God's way, you will succeed. You will prosper.

As you read this, you may doubt what I'm saying. The problem is not in what I'm saying, but in your belief system. Yes, you may love God, yet you may not trust what His Word says. You must learn to destroy the poverty mind-set inside. If you don't think you can prosper in anything—finances, relationships, or careers—then you won't. To begin this process of changing your mental framework, you need to constantly feed yourself in the Word. Learn what God says about you and your life. Learn that God has designed you to succeed and that He takes pleasure in seeing you prosper. Before you begin reworking your mind-set to understand that God wants you to prosper, pray.

Dear Lord,

I have to feed myself with thoughts of success. Even if a curveball comes my way, I'm guaranteed success because the Lord is my helper. I need to feed myself with successful thoughts. I am the sum total of my thoughts. In other words, I become whatever I'm constantly thinking. If I think I will succeed in business, then I will. But if I'm unsure whether I will succeed or think I won't, for whatever reason, then I won't succeed, even if I try. So I must guard my thoughts and always think I will succeed in everything, no matter what I do, where I am, or what the circumstances may be. If my thoughts are those of success, progress, prosperity, peace, joy, and all good things, then my words and actions will correspond according to my thinking. I must, therefore, constantly think on good things, speak good things, and live good things, believing that success will come in every avenue of my life, regardless of what takes place around me.

Furthermore, nothing I think should be outside the realm of my Creator, my God, my divine helper, because without Him any form of success will still fail. With Him in the midst of all my thoughts, words, and actions, however, the success I reap will be full of joy. Lord, help me to keep my thoughts in line with Your thoughts; therefore, my words and ways will come into alignment with Your will. Amen.

Pray the Word

While you're acting on your financial plan, ignite your work of faith with the power of God's Word. Nothing is as powerful as the Word of God. Knowing what God says to you about your finances and constantly reminding yourself about it through prayer and confession of that Word builds your faith in God and keeps all things in perspective and on the road to success. If you give thanks to God and others, feed yourself with the Word of God, and pray the Word while taking steps in your financial management to keep your money in alignment with God's will, you will see progress. Here are a few Scriptures I use to guard my heart and keep my mind focused on the One who provides all.

Financial success:

"For you know the grace of our Lord Jesus Christ, that though He was rich, yet for your sakes He became poor, that you through His poverty might become rich."

—2 Corinthians 8:9

"But his delight is in the law of the Lord, and in His law he meditates day and night. He shall be like a tree planted by the rivers of water, that brings forth its fruit in its season, whose leaf also shall not wither; and whatever he does shall prosper."

—Psalm 1:2–3

Income generation:

"And you shall remember the Lord your God, for it is He who gives you power to get wealth, that He may establish His covenant which He swore to your fathers, as it is this day."

—Deuteronomy 8:18

"For exaltation comes neither from the east nor from the west nor from the south. But God is the Judge: He puts down one, and exalts another."

—Psalm 75:6–7

Tithing:

"Bring all the tithes into the storehouse, that there may be food in My house, and try Me now in this,' says the Lord of hosts, 'If I will not open for you the windows of heaven and pour out for you such blessing that there will not be room enough to receive it. And I will rebuke the devourer for your sakes, so that he will not destroy the fruit of your ground, nor shall the vine fail to bear fruit for you in the field,' says the Lord of hosts; 'And all nations will call you blessed, for you will be a delightful land,' says the Lord of hosts."

—Malachi 3:10–12

Giving:

"And God is able to make all grace abound toward you,

that you, always having all sufficiency in all things, may have an abundance for every good work."

—2 Corinthians 9:8

Spending sensibly:

"Go to the ant, you sluggard! Consider her ways and be wise, which, having no captain, overseer or ruler, provides her supplies in the summer, and gathers her food in the harvest."

—Proverbs 6:6–8

Saving:

"The Lord will command the blessing on you in your storehouses and in all to which you set your hand, and He will bless you in the land which the Lord your God is giving you."

—Deuteronomy 28:8

Investing:

"A good man leaves an inheritance to his children's children, but the wealth of the sinner is stored up for the righteous."

—Proverbs 13:22

Debt freedom:

"The Lord will open to you His good treasure, the heavens, to give the rain to your land in its season, and to bless all the work of your hand. You shall lend to many nations, but you shall not borrow."

—Deuteronomy 28:12

Lending:

"For the Lord your God will bless you just as He promised you; you shall lend to many nations, but you shall not borrow; you shall reign over many nations, but they shall not reign over you."

—Deuteronomy 15: 6

Everyday supply:

"And my God will liberally supply (fill to the full) your every need according to His riches in glory in Christ Jesus."

—Philippians 4:19 (AMP)

"The Lord is my Shepherd [to feed, guide, and shield me], I shall not lack."

—Psalm. 23:1 (AMP)

For whatever ails you in life, you can find an answer in the Word of God. For healing you will find an answer in the Word. For relationship issues you will find an answer in the Word. For financial needs you will find an answer in the Word. And for whatever human issues you struggle with, God has the answer in His Word. Search the Scriptures. Find and read books about finances. Use the Word to heal your thinking, to change your actions, and to change your life.

SUCCESS KEYS

Some things in life we can't live without. We have certainly established that we need the Lord Jesus in our lives. As we endeavor to align our finances to the will of God, however, we need some principles or keys to help us achieve success. Having these keys will help us become great financial stewards.

I pray for and daily strive to have these keys operating in my life because they (1) help me grow in character, (2) remind me to totally rely not on my feeble strength, but on the Almighty God, and (3) keep me focused on my goals, especially when life gets tough. They also remind me that as I work toward any dream or goal, success is a learning journey achieved daily as I stay connected to God.

You will notice that, as you continue this financial journey and your walk of life, you will need these keys to progress and succeed.

The Fear of the Lord

The fear of the Lord is not a trembling dread of God, but a reverence and respect for God and who He is. When you fear the Lord, you honor and worship the Almighty God, your Creator. You are consciously aware that God is always present and you live your life to please Him in every moment.

What does the fear of the Lord have to do with success in life or your finances? Well, if you want knowledge, it begins by fearing God (Prov. 1:7). If you need wisdom, it also begins with fearing the Lord (Prov. 9:10). To become a great financial steward, you need wisdom and knowledge; the start of such soundness comes from fearing God. The fear of the Lord is to both hate and shun evil. When you fear the Lord, you find get-rich-quick schemes to be detestable and avoid them. The fear of the Lord keeps money in its proper perspective, as Proverbs 15:16 says: "Better is a little with the fear of the Lord, than great treasure with trouble." The fear of God is far more necessary and important than the amount of money you possess.

Actually, while on this journey to align your finances to God's will, you will learn to fear the Lord! You will show reverence and honor to Him as you put your financial house in order. Whatever you do in this world, always recognize and acknowledge the presence of God and His lordship over your life. At all times and in all ways reverence God.

Knowledge

We need to be knowledgeable about our lives—our careers, our finances, and our understanding of how to be loving spouses or effective parents. We should always be in learning mode. To know the facts, truths, or principles of personal finances will bring us closer to financial empowerment. Learning or becoming familiar with the subject matter of money and how it works is necessary for success.

Gaining knowledge should be preferred above money (Prov. 8:10). In other words, to possess money but lack knowledge about how to manage it often results in the lack of money. Good or sound knowledge will help us increase and fill our homes "with all precious and pleasant riches" (Prov. 24:4). Knowing how to spend our money (how and where to find what we need for our homes) is a good thing.

I admire some dear friends who have the gift of shopping around. Their house is absolutely beautiful—everybody's dream home is filled with beautiful things. But I have much to learn from this couple. I learned that I should never buy anything on credit and that I can purchase floor models of some of the best brands at rock-bottom prices. Their home is filled with precious and pleasant things gained by waiting, using layaway plans, saving, negotiating, paying cash, and not swiping credit cards. Something about this method is beneficial—the peace of knowing that they owe no one for anything in their home.

Knowledge also increases our strength or power (Prov. 24:5), for without it we can struggle through life. First and foremost we must seek the knowledge of God. He can teach us (Ps. 94:10).

You may not think you can learn anything from God, but His Word alone is filled with knowledge for living. He can also give you knowledge to learn any subject; for example, he taught Daniel and his friends literature (Dan. 1:17). If He can do that, certainly He can teach you about money—the Word has a lot on this subject.

You can also gain knowledge by reading other books on finances, reviewing articles on the Internet, or taking a course or two on the subject. As you gain this knowledge, God will give you the understanding and wisdom needed to apply it to your life.

Understanding

We all need understanding, which is part of the learning process. First, we acquire information, but without being able to mentally process it, that information is useless to us. Understanding is being able to comprehend information or discern people or circumstances. The understanding of two people on a matter, however, can be quite different. This is why we need to ask God for understanding. He is able to give our minds clarity so we can correctly understand and discern what is happening around us.

Life seems to get more and more complicated every day—it offers a constant influx of information, and we need to learn whether to receive it. Technology and financial options are frequently evolving; in fact, our world is constantly changing. If we want to live successfully in this world, we need the spirit of understanding.

The sons of Issachar understood the times in which they lived. They knew it was the right time to make David king of Israel. They saw he was becoming stronger, while the house of Judah was becoming weaker. So the sons of Issachar—both the two hundred chiefs "and all their brethren . . . at their command" (1 Chron. 12:22)—joined ranks with David's army. Understanding helps us to act wisely at the right time and in the right season, thus bringing success to us.

If you lack understanding about how to manage your finances now and in the years ahead, ask God. Seek God before you make any decisions, and He will give you guidance. Trusting in your own understanding has no point; you need understanding from God—that is what will bring you success (Prov. 3:5–6).

David was in constant conversation with God about which wars to fight and how to fight them, and he never went into battle without consulting God. Life is a battlefield, and we must wisely and carefully choose which battles we should engage in. If you and I want to achieve any success in life, we must do so with God directing our paths all the way.

We can all agree that understanding what to do—or not to do—can be a daunting task sometimes. With so much information available to us, we can become overwhelmed and even more uncertain about the decisions we need to make. God's Word is filled with so much about money that we should always make it the starting point when we need to make a decision concerning finances and certainly any area of our lives. The entrance of God's Word in our hearts will give us understanding (Ps. 119:130). We must also use the Word to enlighten our understanding in financial matters and always seek God first.

Wisdom

Wisdom is the capacity to do the right thing at the right time using biblical principles. It is being able to view life from God's perspective and acting accordingly. When you are knowledgeable about your finances and understand what's happening around you, you can act wisely. Wisdom, therefore, is right application of what you know and understand. It's being and living in alignment with God's will.

Wisdom is beneficial to your whole life. It gives life to your soul as well as confidence and peace (Prov. 3:21–26). Wisdom protects you from making rash or emotional decisions and from being drawn into evil schemes (Prov. 2:10–15; 14:15–16). Wisdom is a gift from God, and His Spirit can fill you with the ability to be gifted in your work (Ex. 31:3, 6). God stores away sound and godly wisdom and reveals it to you so your life may be all He planned for you.

Wisdom comes from our heavenly Father whenever and wherever we are in life. When we ask Him for wisdom, He will give liberally because He loves us (James 1:5). Therefore ask Him to give you financial wisdom.

Favor

Favor is unfair, but we all need it sometimes throughout our lives. Favor is being given preferential treatment above someone else. It comes to us vertically from the Father and horizontally from others. When He was living on the earth, Jesus had favor (Luke 2:52).

Favor is an act of kindness given to us, not because of our great qualities but because God touches someone's heart to go out of his or her way to bless us. Favor is God moving the heart of men to bless us often in unexpected and unusual ways. It is an act of good will. For example, while doing business, someone may choose to charge us less than the stated full price on the invoice, or maybe at work we are promoted before someone else who thought he or she was guaranteed the promotion. Joseph was a slave, yet he was promoted twice to higher positions of responsibility and respected by those he was given authority over (Gen. 39:4–6, 21–24). He was a foreigner, slave, and prisoner, yet God favored him. God not only favored him, but blessed those whose blessing promoted him.

I have seen this favor in my life. When I migrated to Canada, I had work already in place because my employer had spoken well of me. I received a major salary increase I had been asking God for when my former employer hired me. In a condo purchase, I asked for and received completely new flooring and a closing date one month earlier than the initial agreement—all because of God's favor.

You need favor in your life. Before you step out to begin your day, ask God for favor. As you aim to manage your money His way—whether you're negotiating payment arrangements with creditors or selling your products or services—you need favor. Favor demonstrates the kindness of God and others to you. Favor will help bring you success in all your endeavors.

Discipline

From a biblical perspective, discipline is instruction in the will of God enforced by godly correction. As Christians, we discipline ourselves through the study and practice of the Word of God to live in accordance with God's Word. Discipline, which requires time and effort, can be unpleasant at times, but it is needed for our growth as people and Christians. Financial discipline is part of our growth process as Disciples of Christ. For example, financial discipline may be needed in the area of spending. We may need to evaluate where we spend our money and determine areas where we need to cut back, especially if we purchase more of our want-to-haves than our need-to-haves.

Any initial effort to become disciplined in any area—for example, keeping physically fit or managing our finances—can be challenging, but will reap great rewards in our lives.

Discipline corrects us; it keeps us from going in the wrong direction or acting on an impulse. Sometimes God disciplines or corrects us if we are outside His will or moving in the wrong direction. Whether through His Word as we study it, through circumstances, or through the instruction of someone else, God proves His love for us when He disciplines us. As a Father, God desires what is best for His children and sometimes gives harsh instruction to prevent calamity (Heb. 12:5–11). Another benefit of discipline comes from the effort it takes to study, understand, and apply the principles of what we've learned. As a disciple of Christ, the study of the Word of God keeps God's purpose for us ever in the forefront of our thinking. Also, as we study the principles of personal finances, we become ever thoughtful, implementing the good principles into our daily money management. Therefore, discipline keeps us focused on practicing what is right based on what God's Word says and living daily in a way that pleases God.

If your finances are not as they should be, you need to exercise financial discipline in how to manage your finances. So how can you become financially disciplined? First, study and follow the instructions found in the Word of God. Second, supplement the Word by reading books or articles on personal finance and by listening to financial news. Third, put into practice what you've learned, especially in those areas where you may be most challenged. For example, you may need to increase your savings, reduce your debt, limit your spending, or give more. Fourth, you should recruit a trusted friend who is knowledgeable in finances or a financial professional who can assist you on this journey by keeping you accountable. Finally, as you go through the process of change, stay focused on the goal, aligning your finances to God's will. Therefore, lean on Him for instruction and direction, and He will help you.

Diligence

Diligence and discipline go hand in hand. We need discipline to be diligent. The Word of God emphasizes the need to be diligent in whatever we do—in seeking the Lord and in the work we do daily. So what does being diligent mean? It means the constant and earnest effort to accomplish a task or goal. Diligence is persistence in hard work. It is the opposite of being lazy and procrastinating. Diligence means working hard and continuing to work until we've completed whatever we're doing.

One plus to being diligent is that we keep our focus on the goal. Long after the excitement of an initial project, such as revamping our finances, has passed, we keep working at it because diligent people see the end of the project even before they reach it. The reward of diligence is sweet to the soul; we reap the pleasure of an accomplished goal and bask in it (Prov. 12:27), while those who are lazy still wish and achieve nothing (Prov. 13:4). Another wonderful benefit of being diligent is knowing that our plans are guaranteed to bring abundance. Our plans will prosper and produce the results we want (Prov. 21:5). Diligence also leads to riches (Prov. 10:4) and positions of authority (Prov. 12:24). Diligence rewards.

I'm sure you can look back at your life and see where you've benefited by being diligent. It took diligence for me to complete several courses of study to obtain a degree or a certificate. I needed diligence to see my plan for a new home become a reality.

To see your financial goals and other life goals happen will take continued diligence. If you want to accomplish anything in life, you will need diligence to do it. Therefore, as you examine yourself, seek God's help if you lack diligence in any area. Focus on the goal, the prize, and keep diligently working towards it.

KEEP IT REAL

I think the key to keeping all this money business in perspective is to keep it real. What do I mean by that?

1. Be Realistic

You may be eager to get things on the road, so to speak. You may be keen to save more, give more, and spend a lot less. However, avoid outlandish goals. For example, saving a million dollars in one year is outlandish if your current annual income is only sixty-five thousand dollars.

God is a real God too. Yes, He can (and does) do great and mighty things in our lives. But we often need to learn to start with small beginnings before bigger blessings come. God wants to see us handle the small before He blesses us with the big.

2. Be Encouraged

Any goal worth accomplishing often proves challenging. If this book has challenged you to bring order to your financial life, every effort you make is well worth it. Be aware, however, that discouragement can come. Therefore, learn to encourage yourself in the Lord. Also encourage yourself by reviewing your goals frequently. Post them where you can see them easily and talk about them daily. Tell yourself you can make it: "I can do all things through Christ who gives me strength. Yes, I can make it. Yes, I can save $_____ every month. Yes, I can buy a new home by _____ (fill in the date)." Engage in positive self talk and encourage yourself with God's Word. Keeping faith in God will help you and strengthen you through tough times.

3. Be Aligned

We should keep aligned to God's Word and always be a student of it. We all have a tendency to forget the Word of God, not necessarily because we want to, but because the Enemy may tempt us to. Distractions come along to steer us off track from our goals.

Have you ever noticed that after a church service people will tell you what a great and powerful message they heard, yet they can't give you any details about the sermon? Every word of God you hear is meant to bring growth. Like a plant, you need water, sunshine, and other natural elements to grow. The Word of God keeps you aligned with God's will. As you take this journey to improve your finances, let the Word of God be ever present to keep you on the right track.

4. Be Looking Up

"I will lift up my eyes to the hills—from whence comes my help? My help comes from the Lord, who made heaven and earth"

—Ps. 121:1–2

No man is an island and can do everything on his own and reap success. There is no such thing as being a self-made man or woman. We all need help. For us as believers, our first and foremost help is from the Lord Himself. The One who created heaven and earth is the One to whom we should always run for help. According to a Barbadian proverb, "God don't come, but He does send." Help comes from God in many ways. We can attest to times when we cried to God for help because we lacked enough to meet our needs, and God provided through someone else.

I have experienced the blessing of having bills paid on my behalf because I looked to God for help in prayer. I can testify to God's help when I lacked enough food in the cupboards, yet He made sure we didn't go hungry. I can say for sure that, through the ups and downs of life along with financial challenges, looking up to God has been my greatest triumph. God has always come through for me, and He can also do that for you. Just look up and cry out to God for help in whatever area of finances you have a need, and He will help you.

So keep everything in perspective by keeping it real.

CHAPTER 13

Righteousness and Riches: They Go Together

God delights in the prosperity—in the all-around success—of His saints. Our desire for success needs to be aligned with God's will. God expects us to prosper—to have more than enough to be a blessing to others. A blessed man or woman is a blessing to others.

Praise the Lord! Blessed is the man who fears the Lord, Who delights greatly in His commandments. His descendants will be mighty on earth; the generation of the upright will be blessed. Wealth and riches will be in his house, and his righteousness endures forever. Unto the upright there arises light in the darkness; He is gracious, and full of compassion, and righteous. A good man deals graciously and lends; He will guide his affairs with discretion. Surely he will never be shaken; the righteous will be in everlasting remembrance. He will not be afraid of evil tidings; His heart is steadfast, trusting in the Lord.

His heart is established; He will not be afraid, until he sees his desire upon his enemies. He has dispersed abroad, He has given to the poor; His righteousness endures forever; His horn will be exalted with honor. The wicked will see it and be grieved; He will gnash his teeth and melt away; the desire of the wicked shall perish.

—Psalm 112:1–10

IN GOD YOU TRUST AND PROSPER

God delights in the prosperity—the all-around success—of His saints. Yes, God delights in our prosperity. It pleases Him when we have more than enough and are good stewards as wealth creators and distributors. God expects us to prosper, to have more than enough to be a blessing to others.

As we walk through Scripture, we find many examples of men and women who walked with God and also were wealthy. Abraham had so much that his possessions and Lot's could not be contained in the same piece of land. Many would have considered Isaac crazy to make the investment he did during the time of famine, but his obedience to God caused him to become a very prosperous man. Jacob, whom no one would trust, learned to relate to God through his years of wandering, and God prospered him tremendously. Israel fled a place of slavery as a wealthy nation (Ex. 12:35-36). They had so much to give to God when the tabernacle was being built that Moses had to stop them from bringing more gifts.

David, a man who loved God, prepared great and precious riches for the building of the temple. Solomon continued from where his father left off, contributing more than his father and the people of Israel did. According to estimates, the temple would be valued in the thousands of millions to trillions of dollars.

Then there's Job; the one who loved God and shunned evil was a very wealthy man in his day (Job 1:5, 8). Yes, he lost it all, but as he sought God and prayed for his friends, God restored double what he had. Jesus came to this earth, and He too was prosperous—he had enough to take care of Himself and those who followed Him. Never once do we read of Jesus struggling to find a meal to eat or a place to sleep. Though His life wasn't as conventional as ours (house, car, family), He lacked nothing. When it was time to pay the temple tax, He astonished Peter by locating hidden riches in the mouth of a fish to take care of His financial responsibilities. These examples teach us that riches and righteousness go together.

Therefore, you need to realign your thinking to be success oriented just like your Father God. Never believe that lack is for you. As you walk uprightly before your Father, where no lack exists, do not accept lack, but rather disallow it. Your Father has great abundance and has already provided what you need for life and godliness. Use the power, the anointing God has given to you to create wealth. Walk as a blessed man or woman in every way. Be a blessing to others.

What others are saying about FINANCIAL EMPOWERMENT:

Understanding personal finance and having the discipline to manage a budget and save for the future are key factors toward achieving personal life goals, but knowlege and understanding about our spiritual well-being and our creator who makes all things possible are even more fundamental to our overall prosperity. This book reinforces the knowledge of how we are blessed and become wealthy through a commitment to and belief in God, who is our source.

—Carol A. Pitt, Caribbean Chapters Publishing

I found Financial Empowerment to be very Bible-centered, informative and challenging especially at a time when money is such a major issue with world-wide economic problems. It's a very practical guide to help the reader glean financial principles in times like these.

—Pastor Cavour Blackman, New Wine Ministries

As a reviewer of numerous Christian publications, I can attest that "Financial Empowerment" is exceptional. Carmichael's 27 years of Christian service echoes page after page. I was impressed with the depth and breadth that she lovingly demonstrated about specific areas—

God's assignment of work, leaving an inheritance and using your money to help others. Readers will have their minds renewed and their finances restored.

—Danita Dyess, Readers' Favorite

Author's Note

Thank you so much for joining me on this journey of **Financial Empowerment: Realign Your Finances to God's Will**. I hope that your leave with some ideas on how you can change your financial situation using God's principles as well as some of the tips I've shared. Being financial empowered is an ongoing process and one that should be done with the Master guiding you along the way.

Feel free to send me an email at pamc@pamelavcarmichael.com to share how your finances and your Christian life have changed through this book. You can also visit my blog at http://www.pamelavcarmichael.com.

Share your financial empowerment stories at:

http://www.pamelavcarmichael.com/financial-empowerment

Financial Empowerment Resources

Special Bonus Offer

You will receive a FREE complementary e-course:

5 Tips to Financial Empowerment God's Way

It's not enough just to have this book in hand, read it and move on without implementing some of what you learned here. You have to continue on the road to Godly financial empowerment. In this free e-course, I will walk you through some action steps that lead to good money management that will bring positive returns into your finances and your life.

Get your copy now at:

http://www.pamelavcarmichael.com/financial-empowerment/5-tips-ecourse

Note: This ebook is NOT free to sell or give away to others. Thanks for understanding.

If you want to go deeper and really live financially empowered as God desires for you, check out Pamela's website for upcoming titles, courses and programs

http://www.pamelavcarmichael.com/

Wishing You Financial Empowerment God's Way

About the Author

Award-winning self-published author, PAMELA CARMICHAEL, is a financial services professional with over 10 years experience. In her Christian walk, the burning question to God has always been: Why do Christians struggle with finances? With a desire to see Christians grow in the area of personal financial management, she embarked on writing *Financial Empowerment: Realign Your Finances to God's Will*. She hopes that you will grow and become financially empowered as you apply God's principles to your personal financial management strategies.

Pamela has a passion to see God's people move from struggle to success not only financially but in all areas of life. Visit Pamela's blog, at http://www.pamelavcarmichael.com to be encouraged to live your best in Christ.

Connect with Pamela:

Facebook –
https://www.facebook.com/PamelaVCarmichaelAuthor

Twitter –
https://twitter.com/pamvcarmichael

Google Plus –
https://plus.google.com/111618081837667826781/posts/p/pub

www.ingramcontent.com/pod-product-compliance
Lightning Source LLC
Chambersburg PA
CBHW021219090426
42740CB00006B/287